A Beautiful Resistance

Left Sacred

Gods&Radicals

contact: editor@godsandradicals.org

godandradicals.org

Cover art, design, and layout: Li Pallas

bureau.lipallaslovesyou.com

Editorial Team: Lia Hunter, Rhyd Wildermuth

Additional Editing: Cat Mead

TABLE OF CONTENTS

About A Beautiful Resistance

A Beautiful Resistance is the Gods&Radicals Journal.
Everything We Already Are (November 2015) was our first issue, edited by Rhyd Wildermuth.
The Fire Is Here (May, 2016) was our second issue, edited by Lorna Smithers
Left Sacred (February, 2017) is our third issue, edited by Rhyd Wildermuth and Lia Hunter

About Gods&Radicals

Gods&Radicals is a non-profit anti-capitalist Pagan publisher and a Site of Beautiful Resistance, founded on
1 May, 2015.
In addition to A Beautiful Resistance, we have published the following works:
A Pagan Anti-Capitalist Primer (March, 2016) by Alley Valkyrie and Rhyd Wildermuth
Pagan Anarchism (November, 2016) by Christopher Scott Thompson
Information about ordering our publications can be found at godsandradicals.org/publications
Writer queries should be directed to editor@godsandradicals.org
Visit our website at:

godsandradicals.org

Resist beautifully!

FOREWORD

Margaret Killjoy

These are the moments we're made for, you and I.

We were not born for easy lives, we were not born for happy lives. We were born to, in the words of Octavia Butler, shape change and be shaped by it in turn. Because God, according to Butler, is Change.

❉ ❉ ❉

There's a scene in a movie I love, a scene I think about far too often. The movie is Edelweisspiraten. It's about the Edelweiss Pirates, a youth subculture from Weimar Germany that started as a sort of cultural resistance to the authoritarian and patriotic norms of Nazi Germany and transformed into an autonomous guerrilla resistance force as the situation became more dire.

At one point, our heroes—let's be honest about what they are, heroes—are raiding a Nazi storeroom. One of the Pirates is terrified. He's freaking out. "C'mon guys, we've got enough, it's time to go."

That's me. I'm the scared kid. I'm fucking terrified of what's to come. I'm fucking terrified because I know I'm going to fight and I know that I'm not constitutionally built for conflict. I know both of these things because of years of experience in fighting for what I believe—sometimes physically—and the years of anxiety and therapy and PTSD that have been the result.

Despite the toll that fighting has taken on me, I wouldn't go back and change a thing. These are the lives we were made to live. The work we do, in any field, will slowly destroy our bodies. I wear my trauma like I wear my tattoos and I will not let myself be ashamed of either.

Even if you're the kid who's scared shitless, be the kid who's scared shitless who still throws down.

❉ ❉ ❉

Cultural shifts are the long game of revolution. When I write a novel, my hope is that one day someone will read it, consider my point of view, and adopt the parts of it that make sense to them. Since every action is a spell cast for more of the same, writing books is a spell cast for more people to write books. Books are not revolutions. But ideas can spread this way—hopefully less through individual "great" works that influence everyone as much as through many books with many ideas that permeate through numerous iterations by numerous authors and artists of all sorts.

Cultural shifts are the long game, but they are starting to bear fruit. We're starting to win some major battles. Ideas that only a half a generation ago belonged only to the radical fringe—like a culture of consent or the self-determination of gender—are mainstream.

The rise of reactionary politics—exemplified in the English-speaking West by Brexit and Donald Trump—is just that: a reaction. It is the last, desperate attempt by a dying cultural force. It's an attempt we need to take seriously. It might still win. But while the reactionaries have been the ones to move the war into the political realm, it was a war we started. We started it by challenging the cultural status quo. We started it by daring to be ourselves, by daring to be free.

LEFT SACRED

Cultural shifts are the long game. It's time to focus on the short game: politics. Fortunately, the immediacy of the situation removes electoral politics—perhaps the most banal and impotent expression of politics—from our toolbox. When I say politics, I simply mean "the ways in which we organize power within our society." It's time to take that power ourselves and spread that power out to others. It's time to transform our aesthetic cultures into cultures of resistance. It's time for action.

Every action you take is a spell cast for more of that action. Defend people. Stand up to bigots. Hospitalize bigots if need be, or maybe get hospitalized in the attempt. Spells are often costly. That's fine. They should be. The work we do might destroy us.

✲ ✲ ✲

For decades now, at least in the Western world, politics have remained locked in place. The status quo was a pin thrust through the heart of our society, sticking us in one spot on the board of possibilities. Elections, then, were like a mob of people gathered around the pin, carefully unsticking it, and shifting it by scant inches before thrusting it firmly back into place.

That pin is unstuck. It can move in any direction, any distance.

It was our enemies—let's be honest and call them what they are, enemies—who unstuck that pin. But their hold on it isn't secure. If we act, now, we can take hold of our lives and our culture and make a break with the awful reality of the old status quo, all while fighting those who would turn the bad-dream world we're used to into a living fucking nightmare.

My metaphor of a pin in a map falls apart pretty quickly, though, because it's not a single pin. It's millions, billions of pins: each of us as individuals and communities. As an anarchist, my job isn't to move every single pin—every single person, every single community—to the position I hope to occupy on the political map. My job is move myself and my community. My job is to help others move themselves to where they hope to be.

An anarchist world isn't a world in which every living person calls themself an anarchist. An anarchist world is a world of possibilities, in which no institutional power can force communities and individuals into subservience.

✲ ✲ ✲

These coming years probably won't go well for us, but let's be real: on a long enough timeline, nothing does.

We've been preparing for years and decades. We've been laying the seeds of resistance. It's time to see what we can harvest.

I hope we are ready, because it is time.

Margaret Killjoy

Margaret Killjoy is a gender-deviant author and editor currently based in the Appalachian mountains. Her most recent book is an anarchist utopia called A Country of Ghosts. Her next book, The Lamb Will Slaughter the Lion, is forthcoming from Tor.com in 2017. She blogs at birdsbeforethestorm.net.

A BEAUTIFUL RESISTANCE

INTRODUCTION:
Left Sacred

On the 19th of June, 1937, an exhibition opened in the city of Munich. Called *Die Ausstellung "Entartete Kunst,"*[1] it housed paintings, sculptures, and other works carefully curated to warn against the scourge of degenerate art. Amongst the stated goals of the exhibition was the "deliberate and calculated onslaught upon the very essence and survival of art itself," along with "the common roots of political anarchy and cultural anarchy."[2]

Included in the collection were works by the Swiss painter Paul Klee. One hundred and two of his paintings had been seized, though a rather famous one survived in the hands of the Marxist mystic philosopher, Walter Benjamin. The piece was called *Angelus Novus,* and Benjamin would later write about it, without revealing that it was in his possession. Its angular and stark depiction inspired his famous conception of the "Angel of History."

Before Walter Benjamin's attempted escape through Spain to the United States, the mystic had entrusted the painting to his friend, the student of the transgressive Sacred, Georges Bataille. The painting itself is transgressive, an incomprehensible Sacred, wishing, as Benjamin wrote, "to stay, awaken the dead, and make whole what has been smashed."[3] But the angel cannot: its wings are caught, it must continue on this new wind, leaving the wreckage of history behind, progressing not towards some great evolutionary goal, but merely away from the ruins of the past.

That the painting was seen as degenerate makes the Angel of History more fascinating. The Fascist current of history, the one which awakens strongly now in our present, cannot abide degeneracy and sees it everywhere. Fallen, fallen are we, decadent pale shadows of our once great glory. Our blood is too mixed, our house too messy, our genders and sex too confused, our borders unfenced, the land crowded with foreigners, our children dirtied by the melanin of others. Make America Great Again, restore the Empire, save Liberal Democracy, uphold the rule of law, return to us an innocence that never was.

Where the Fascists see former glory, the Angel of History, passed hand-to-hand by degenerate leftists, sees only wreckage. Walter Benjamin would not survive the Nazi attempt to restore Germany to its mythic former glory, but the Angelus Novus did. One even suspects the Angel of History did have time to awaken some of the dead. Benjamin haunts these pages, as does Bataille's search for a transgressive Sacred, as does the *Angelus Novus* itself, all collected in the messy, fierce, resurrection of a degenerate left sacred.

What is a sacred left? What is left of the sacred? What is the left sacred? These are the interweaving themes of this third issue of *A Beautiful Resistance,* watched over by the Angel of History, its wings forced open by a wind from another world.

> ⮑ A goddess of the poor and outcast speaks in Erynn Rowan Laurie's **Brig Ambu.**
>
> ⮑ Gods topple off thrones in Rhyd Wildermuth's **Awakening Against What's Awakened.**
>
> ⮑ An office window opens and love awakens in **The Necromancer,** by Left Eye

1   German: *Degenerate Art Exhibition*
2   From the introduction to the exhibition.
3   Thesis IX of Walter Benjamin's *On the Concept of History*

- The wild fights with fang and claw in **After Procopius**, by Lorna Smithers.
- Rot is decomposed and grown into new life in Nina George's **Modern Sin-Eaters**.
- Nimue Brown explores a line-less cartography in **The Druidry of Mapping**.
- William Hawes sees in pre-linear time the path to the future in **The Reawakening of Tribal Consciousness**.
- **In Bell Unrung**, Lia Hunter mourns the toll of what we do not embrace.
- Anthony Rella's **Gods of My Ancestors** contemplates the messy history of blood and deity.
- An Angel whispers, a carpet is stained, in Hunter Hall's **Yellow Tape & White Carpet**.
- Chimeras and hybrid monsters lead us to the world outside of fences in Finnchuill's **The Impure Object of The Left Sacred**.
- Revolution smells like swamp rot and rum in Dr. Bones' **Fear & Loathing At The Crossroads**.
- All the beauty of the many-gendered dead sing in **Rocket's Prayer to the Mother(s)**.
- A writer scribbles final notes to the future in Yvonne Aburrow's **The Safe House**.
- Sean Donahue dances with the Angel in **Against the Winds of History**.
- And in **Solidarity Networks**, we outline a strategy for all those wondering 'what next' as fascism rises in the nations of the world.

This issue was co-edited by Lia Hunter and Rhyd Wildermuth, and also proudly displays the artwork and photography of Lois Cordelia, Marion le Bourhis, Christopher Delange, and Brianna Bliss, with the cover brilliance of Li Pallas.

May all that is messy, degenerate, unrestrained, and feral about you awaken, and may you dance in the winds of history.

experiences-called-gods, too. Though sometimes I use others. Brighid is the Lady of the Hearth, though sometimes of the Flame, or of Tears, or the Rain. Brân's the Raven King, and also the Guardian at the Gate of the Dead. Ceridwen's sometimes the Huntress, and sometimes Gwyn Ap Nudd Hunts, too.

Arianrhod's the Silver Wheel, and a lot of other names I don't really understand yet. She avoids comprehension more than the others. When a lover bit my nipples until they started to bleed, I understood something about her I still don't get but feel again sometimes. When I see that pattern of light-on-water, I know a part of my mind awakens and understands. It just refuses to explain to the rest of me.

Gods On Thrones

Gods occupy a space of human meaning. When something strange happens, fortuitous or synchronistic, and when that happens to coincide with what I generally ascribe to the activity of the gods, I am connecting something to the gods by a thread called Meaning. Light dances on water a certain way and I think of Arianrhod. My consciousness seems to expand and yet become more porous into the land around me and I think Brân.

But the gods occupy a different space from other things to which we connect meaning. We usually call that place 'Sacred,' rather than mundane or normal. When I pour out offerings to Arianrhod, it's a sacred thread of meaning, a sort of special category of meaning set apart from all the others. And though we tend to think of that sacred as out of reach of the political, it's never been the case.

Kings, emperors, chiefs, and other human authorities have always ruled by the blessing of the divine, be that gods, God, or another sacred realm outside the reach of material influence. In the present, govern-

Sometimes I feel a hand on the back of my neck, breath in my ear.

ments gain consent to rule by the will of the people; 500 years ago, kings ruled by the will of God and the blessing of the Church; in non-Christian areas, kings claimed to rule through the blessing of the land or the gods.

That space the sacred occupies in political realms is also a realm of meaning, and is the foundation of Authority. A king derives his power from God not because God grants him that authority, but because those he rules over see God as a meaningful thing. Within a society where God is thought to exist, and where God is a pervasive, inescapable thing of meaning, the King who claims such blessing is now backed up by an entire Order of Meaning birthed by that God. How a king is able to convince the rest of us that God has given him Divine Right is of course complicated, helped along by already-existing institutions which maintain the Order of Meaning at which that God is at the head. Violence helps, too.

While a traditional anarchist or Marxist (or even just an atheist) might protest that the God at the head of such an Order of Meaning is merely fictional or constructed, this doesn't actually change the power of the God. As long as enough people within a society believe that there is such a God, and that such a God also grants sovereignty to leaders, and that others (priests, diviners, etc.) can accurately determine that God's will, whether or not the God actually exists is utterly irrelevant. The Order of Meaning is the throne itself, not who sits upon it.

This same mechanism wherein the Sacred sustains an Order of Meaning applies just as much to the Celtic and Germanic ideas of Sacred Kingship as it does to Liberal Democracy's concept of the consent-of-the-governed. Though it may have been Druids or Shamans or Priestesses declaring what the gods willed before, and though it may be elections and the media and politicians declaring what the people will now,

God (or the Sacred) never disappeared as the originator of Authority.

Though many modern Polytheists, Christian Fundamentalists, or Islamic Radicals might use such a knowledge to claim that the Sacred therefore is the true source of Authority (and a source we must return to if we first acknowledge that such a Sacred exists), such a fascistic rush misses another important aspect of the space the Sacred occupies.

While I name certain experiences gods, I do not choose to therefore bow down to them, nor do they demand such a thing. I am aware of Brighid's presence and say hello, or immerse myself into the world of meaning which opens when she's around, but I don't ask her what she therefore demands of me. When something happens which I ascribe to the influence of Arianrhod, I do not kneel or vow to serve her, nor does she ask me to.

It is only certain others, those who teach things about gods, who claim to experience them and draw power from them, who demand that I do such a thing. No god has ever said, "follow me," no deity has ever asked that I give myself over to them in return for riches or power, no sacred being has ever threatened to punish me if I do not do as they say. But plenty of priests and leaders have.

Gods don't demand obedience, but humans certainly do. An employer may certainly use threats to coerce me to do more work, a politician might certainly promise fortune if I grant him consent through ballot, a religious leader has absolutely promised great power and magic if I follow them. And in each of these cases, the demand or threat is backed up by an Order of Meaning in which such obedience is derived from a greater source. Consider:

The employer has more money than I, and the hierarchy which sustains Capitalism is clear.

The politician, once elected, may indeed wield the sort of power that might make me rich, but only because a political system already exists which grants the elected power over the rest of us.

If I believe in the same god(s) of the religious leader and accept their claims to speak on that god(s)'s behalf, I may decide that my personal autonomy is a fair sacrifice.

That is, gods don't demand I bow to them. It is others who demand that things be bowed to or accept an Order of Meaning where bowing to things is what you do.

Those who demand gods be served and worshiped often tell us that it is "because they are gods." This is, of course, no different from a parent saying to a child, "because I said so," or a police officer stating, "it's against the law." In all cases, the reason for the obedience comes from the supposed source of the command itself (parent, god, police). Or, put another way, *Authority must be obeyed because it is Authority, and an Authority is an Authority because an Authority said so.*

> Gods inhabit the spaces we make for them in our world, just as a lover inhabits our consciousness. They become not just an outside thing, but an inside thing, taking root in our heart, our dreams, our thoughts.

The Empty Thrones

Returning to Jung's theory that a thing like a god had possessed the people of Germany, we can start to wonder why there's even a space within us to be possessed in the first place. Remembering that the Sacred has always been used by political powers to create an Order of Meaning in which their authority is secured, we need need ask why such a trick works.

The gods may exist outside ourselves, but the thrones upon which some of us put them don't. Instead, those thrones exist within. Gods inhabit the spaces we make for them in our world, just as a lover inhabits our consciousness. They become not just an outside thing, but an inside thing, taking root in our heart, our dreams, our thoughts.

Put a lover on a throne and their existence is no longer just a beautiful thing to us, but a thing of Order. Put their desires and concerns first above any other, and they no longer just co-create your meaning, they become it. You become subsumed into their existence, a servant, building your life around them rather than with them. It isn't uncommon to hear someone say of their lover, "they are the reason I exist."

It does not matter whether the lover desires such a thing at all. Most wouldn't ascend that throne, if it is to be called love. But it is not really up to them. A lover might decide I am his "all" regardless of whether I'd want to be such a thing (I don't), and I would then experience him as a will-less person, too eager to please, too readily disappointed when I do not fully occupy the ascended place he's made for me.

> No matter how liberated we are, without many others likewise liberated, we stand alone. Our liberation is always contingent on the liberation of others.

It seems it is the same with the gods. Perhaps there are some gods happy to have eager servants willing to absolve their own personality (and responsibility) into them. I do not imagine this does those gods well in the end. For instance, the racists and fascists who invoke Odin and the "northern gods" to justify their hatred seem to do Odin no good; he becomes, like the Christian devil, a shadow-pit into which all the blame for evil is dumped. Worse, such followers do precisely the same thing as the followers of the Christian god did, demanding conformity of belief and killing those who won't submit to their new Order of Meaning.

The thrones upon which we'd put a lover or a god seem to exist regardless of their desires. And that makes me wonder where such things come from—why, really, would we elevate any other being to a place of Authority besides ourselves?

The answer is probably that we've been taught to. We're taught from our youngest years to obey, to acquiesce, to comply. Our parents teach this, our elders and teachers. Police teach this, and tax collectors and jailers. Employers teach this, and journalists and bullies.

Elevate and heed the will of your parents, and you will not get punished. Hearken and obey the words of your teachers and elders, and you will not get shunned or go to detention. Fear and listen to the demands of police, and you will not get shot. Work hard, give up hours of your life and discipline yourself, and you will not get fired and go hungry.

Our societies carve the thrones of Authority into our souls, and there are too many others willing to sit upon them.

Putting gods upon those thrones instead of human leaders may actually seem an attempt at freedom. If Brighid occupies the highest Authority of my life, one might think I'd be less likely to obey others. But she doesn't actually fit in that seat, nor does she seem to want to sit in it. The only way for me to keep her there would be to force her into it, bind her to the armrests, chain her feet to the floor. *Stay there and be my master,* I'd have to say, *Tell me what to do so I am no longer responsible for my actions.*

I don't think she'd take that well.

Others might claim she already sits there, that she sits on their own thrones, that she demands this. One sees this often with certain "war" gods like Odin or The Morrígan, but I have never known those gods to be fond of sitting.

No Masters

It is probably not possible to destroy the thrones. Perhaps once carved from the etheric stone of our wills, the thrones never go away. Taught from birth that someone must always have more say than others, disciplined while still crawling across the floor that some must always be lower and some must always be higher, maybe we can never unlearn this. So perhaps it's best if we sit on those thrones ourselves. I think we usually do anyway, and merely displace our blame and guilt when we do something awful, or something does not turn out well. After all, we choose to obey, we choose to submit, we choose to debase our nature before the will of others.

If we sit on our own thrones, we might better resist those who'd coerce us. When others demand we obey their Authority, they'd have to topple us from our own power. When hatred points to the weak and oppressed as the cause of our own weakness, we'd be strong against such designs. Those thrones are, after all, the very seat of our own power.

The 'Wotanic spirit' that awakened into the world during the rise of Hitler is not much different from the great Authorities that have arisen in any other time. Lockstep obedience, subservience to a greater power, sublimation of individuality, and hatred of difference has inhabited humans many times before, and seem to arise now again.

Against such a thing, only those who know no other authority but their own might stand. But there would need to be many of us, many more than there are now. All the self-actualization in the world will not protect us from bullets or bombs, gas chambers or prison cells. No matter how liberated we are, without many others likewise liberated, we stand alone. Our liberation is always contingent on the liberation of others.

What would the world be like if more of us occupied our own thrones? Where freedom from coercion and the divine right of self-mastery became the primary values of our societies? As long as those with whom I interact are enchained by the will of others, I could only ever be an actualized self alone, if such a thing were even possible. To become more my self, I need others to teach me how they become their selves. To be free from the coercion of others, others around me must know what coercion even is. And here's where the gods, temporarily unseen, resurge back like an immense tide. Beings existing outside our enchainment, needing neither to coerce nor force but merely be: are they not the very ideal of our own freedom?

That we would put them on thrones, enchain their meaning and extract it for our own desire to rule everyone but ourselves: the only result of such a thing is rivers of blood running down streets or ziggurats, slaughter and manacles and camps. But if instead they are guides of our liberation, themselves unchained, themselves unmastered and unmastering, they are exactly what we might need to oppose whatever new thing is awakening in our world.

We already have guides for this sort of thing. The women and men who snuck into factories under the cover of night, smashing the machinery of the rich Capitalists, claimed to follow a spectral king. "No general but Ludd," went their slogan, "did the worker any good." The Whiteboys of Ireland did the same, following a spectral land-goddess, issuing evictions in her name. Not obedience, not submission, but liberation.

Perhaps our gods, like Ludd, will agree to guide us.

But we must be clear whose hands are unshackling others, whose hammers are smashing the machines, and who is actually sitting on those thrones.

RHYD WILDERMUTH

Rhyd is the cofounder and managing editor of Gods&Radicals. He's a writer, a theorist, an anarchist, Pagan, marxist, poet, and a nomad. He writes at Paganarch.com, as well as Fur/Sweat/Flesh (fursweatflesh.org)

LEFT SACRED

THE NECROMANCER

Left Eye

An office window opens,
A child raises his hand
A woman opens the door
A lover starts to smile

An office window opens,
A child raises his hand
A woman opens the door
A lover starts to smile

An office window opens,

It came like a cascade, like the torrent of a waterfall,
it was every unbidden hope and dream,
She emptied the bucket and
A flock of birds pours from the 50th floor onto city streets.
The reams of paper were rain, quenching the longest drought,
And as she scattered them, something inside and underneath cracked and splintered.
The city ruptured like an overripe fruit left in the sun.

A child raises his hand.

Teacher, What is dioxin?
Teacher, How many languages will go extinct today?
Teacher...if the world ends, and there's no one left...what does the cracking of continents sound like?

He asks the teacher if she feels free when she goes to the airport.
He asks the teacher how many of the pencils she bought with her own money.
He asks the teacher, when the night is still and quiet...if she's happy.

A woman opens a door

The cold night gusts inwards, bringing scents of mint and cinnamon,
her first words lace through the zephyr.

A BEAUTIFUL RESISTANCE

It is a promise,
on the other side, wild grass blooms.
it is a battlefield
On the other side is the child she has not borne,
Through the doorway, the arms of the galaxy swirl, slow and incomprehensible,

She looks over her shoulder, at the man standing within,
she says "I'm sorry," and does not look back.

A lover starts to smile,

Dawn flows across the landscape
his eyes are bright, and something rattles in his bones like moths in a lampshade.
He stands on the roof, holding his lover's face in his hands, as the sun comes up
Something boils in his throat, it climbs up his esophagus, slinks through his teeth, and bursts into flight.
He says, "I love you."
I love you.

They will tell you that anarchy is throwing bricks, and not the smallest actions every day of your
life. They will tell you that electricity does not run through your bones like a live wire, begging to be
released,
That divinity is beyond your reach, nonexistent, the domain of the chosen, mediated by your betters.
They will tell anything to the walkers, the ones who trek through the desert and ruin. The singers,
who cannot be caged again,
The dreamers, the seers, the outcasts, the children, the poor, the burning,
The burning,
We are burning in a house of vacuum that loves to die
But at our best, we shimmer while we rot
Hold your god like fire on a windy slope,
clutch this thing of blood and heat to your chest,
Do not let them take it
It is yours,
This world, is yours.

Left Eye

Left Eye is a nomad, currently in league with Paumanok, seeking to constellate the Vox Nemorensis, for the benefit of all sentient beings.

LEFT SACRED

AFTER PROCOPIUS

Lorna Smithers

In his History of the Wars (6AD), the classical historian, Procopius, speaks of a wall dividing Britain:

> Now in the island of Britain the men of ancient times built a long wall, cutting off a large part of it; and the climate and the soil and everything else is not alike on the two sides of it. For to the south of the wall there is a salubrious air, changing with the seasons, being moderately warm in summer and cool in winter... But on the north side everything is the reverse of this, so that it is actually impossible for a man to survive there even a half-hour, but countless snakes and serpents and every other kind of wild creature occupy this area as their own. And, strangest of all, the inhabitants say that if a man crosses this wall and goes to the other side, he dies straightaway... They say, then, that the souls of men who die are always conveyed to this place.[5]

It is my intuition that Procopius was talking about the Antonine Wall, which ran from the Firth of Forth to the Forth of Clyde and formed the northernmost border of the Roman Empire. It was built in 142AD. After only eight years the Romans abandoned it and fled back to Hadrian's Wall. When Roman power broke down in the 5th century, it became the border between the Brythonic Kingdoms of the Old North and the Picts.

In medieval Welsh literature, "the North" has longstanding associations with Annwn, the Brythonic Other-world. After the devastating Battle of Arfderydd, Myrddin Wyllt fled north to Celyddon[6] where he wandered for "ten and twenty years" amongst wild creatures and gwllon: "madmen," "wildmen," or "shades" and learnt the arts of poetry and prophecy.

In Culhwch and Olwen, the earliest Arthurian story, Arthur "came to the North" to rescue Gwythyr ap Greidol[7] and his allies from imprisonment by Gwyn ap Nudd, a ruler of Annwn who contains its "demons." In another episode he "set out to the North" to drain the blood of Orddu, "The Very Black Witch," who dwelt in "Pennant Gofid in the uplands of hell."

"The North" has long-lasting associations with the Otherworld and the Other. These stem from the othering of Annwn (earlier known as Annfwn, "the deep") itself. Prior to Christianity, people lived in reciprocal relationship with their ancestors and the deities of Annwn, making offerings at burial mounds and in ritual pits and shafts. Annwn was close as a prayer.

In the Four Branches of The Mabinogion, which are set in Wales prior to the Roman invasion, Annwn is another kingdom adjacent to and much like ours where marriages and allegiances can be made with its deities. In the post-Roman, militarised, Christianised north, Annwn was identified with hell and its people with demons. They were dislocated from their immanent locations within the landscape and superimposed on territories beyond a wall further north. Arthur was introduced as the defender of Romanised civilisation who kept the other at bay.

Of course, the landscape one side of a wall or any north/south divide is never much different to the other side. The people may be culturally or racially different but they're always human. Annwn and its deities remain close as a prayer within the landscape. Superstitions about what lies beyond the wall result from the false my-

---

5   Cited by August Hunt in *The Mysteries of Avalon* (August Hunt, 2011).
6   The Caledonian Forest.
7   A nobleman of Arthur's court and the father of Arthur's wife, Gwenhwyfar.

A BEAUTIFUL RESISTANCE

thologisations of elites whose power is grounded in fostering fear and creating divisions they claim must be maintained, by them, for the safety of the people.

I believe the othering effects of the Antonine Wall in the writing of Procopius have relevance today. Britain's Leave campaign was founded on the myth that immigrants are responsible for our social and economic ills. This not only others people working hard to contribute to society and the economy but obfuscates the government's failures.

With 52% voting Leave and 48% Remain, a huge wall has been driven between Britain and Europe, Leave and Remain camps, "citizens" and immigrants. It is likely Scotland will hold a second referendum for independence and if this is successful will remain in the EU.

In the face of these divisions it is essential we remember our common ground with those on the other side of the wall rather than listening to those whose power grows from fostering fear and hatred of others. Their blaming of our grievances on immigrants is a myth of the worst kind.

As our government falls apart, now is not the time to look for another Arthur but to reach beyond the wall to our human and non-human neighbours, the living and the dead, to the deities of Annwn, to embrace all others. Let's avoid a return to the standpoint of Procopius.

AFTER PROCOPIUS

"But on the north side... it is actually impossible for a man to survive there even half an hour, but countless snakes and serpents and every other kind of wild creature occupy their area as their own."
—Procopius, The History of the Wars

North of the Wall I am running
from Roman civilisation
from the ones who build straight roads
from the ones who stand in line.

North of the Wall I am running
to greet my madness
a whirlwind of serpents at my heels
torn-out leaves in my hair.

North of the Wall I am running
amongst mad women
streaking bare through the forest
shedding my second skin.

North of the Wall I am running
with every wild creature
a halo of birds around my coming
open-beaked with soaring wings.

North of the Wall I am running
with the hunger of the wolf-pack
howling and slithery-jawed
erupting into fur and paw.

North of the Wall I am running
with the madness of gwyllon:
shadowed men who come as wolves
the greater shadow of Annwn's lord.

LEFT SACRED

North of the Wall I am running
until I don't want to run any more.
In our grove of pine there is silence
and the heartbeat of steady awe.

North of the Wall I stop running
and turn to face my challengers:
roads running on forever
countless rows of spears and shields.

From North of the Wall I return
cloaked in feather and claw.
To breach the gap
and bring down the divide

I am running back from the Wall.

LORNA SMITHERS

Lorna Smithers is an awenydd, Brythonic polytheist and devotee of Gwyn ap Nudd recovering lost stories of the land and myths of forgotten gods and leaving Signposts in the Mist. She is the author of Enchanting the Shadowlands, editor of A Beautiful Resistance: The Fire is Here and a contributor to Awen ac Awenydd, Dun Brython, and Gods & Radicals.

MODERN SIN-EATERS
Nina George

Hel. Spelt with one "l." This is not a place. In Norse mythology, she is a goddess of life and death combining the literal and the metaphorical. Some say she is half skeleton/half person, others that she is half dead/half alive, others yet that she is half black/half white. Most of the other deities found it difficult to look at her and be around her. As a result, she is given the task of attending to the souls of the dead and a place to do this. Not all of the dead though, only those who do not die in battle. The deaths that were seen as dishonourable. It seems that there was only honour to be had by dying in battle. This must have made for some fearsome enemies. That aside, the way Clarissa Pinkola Estes tells it, the dead are brought to Hel by sin-eaters who have eaten the dead and "incubate"[8] them in their bellies. These sin-eaters could be spirits, souls, people, or other animals. They are "carrion-eaters,"[9] like crows or other corvids, other beings we are wary of. Hel receives these incubated dead and shows them "how to live backward. they become younger and younger until they are ready to be reborn and re-released back into life." So, the goddess of death is also the goddess of life. She transforms, and the sin-eaters bring her the souls to transform.

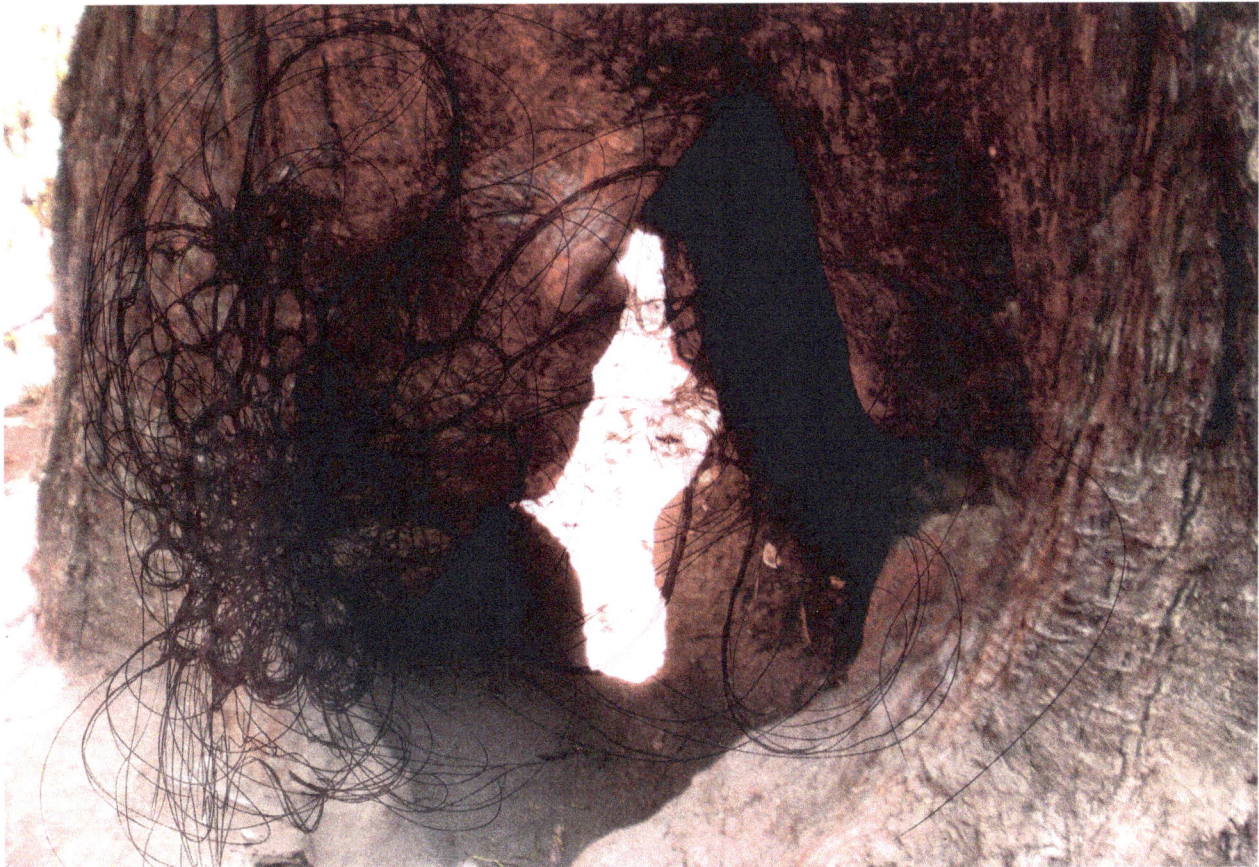

8   Clarissa Pinkola Estes, *Women Who Run with the Wolves.*
9   Clarissa Pinkola Estes, *Women Who Run with the Wolves.*

LEFT SACRED

Sin-eating was a practice carried out fairly regularly from the Middle Ages up until the late 1800s in the U.K. If someone died suddenly and there wasn't the chance for them to confess their sins, a sin-eater would be asked to attend. They would eat a piece of bread that had been passed over or lain on the deceased's chest and drink ale or water that had been passed over the body. Sometimes they were also paid a small amount, too.

In this way, sin-eaters took on the sins of the deceased as their own, thus allowing the dead person to rest in peace. This appears to me to be a sort of voluntary societal scapegoating process. Scapegoating being that which you do not like in yourself being dissociated from and then found in others at a community or individual level. Most people gave those who ate sins a wide berth at other times. Sin-eaters were usually relegated to outcast status. They were mostly poor and disenfranchised people, those whose only meal for the day might be the one taken with a dead person's sins. Or maybe they were paid to go away. Maybe this is survival if you're on the "outside" anyway. Maybe these situations were merely practical necessity. Or is the idea of "choosing" the role meaningless in these situations? However, for every rule set down it often breaks itself, and the last known sin-eater, who died in 1906, was Richard Munslow, a farmer who chose to take up the role locally after he lost three of his children in an outbreak of whooping cough. Maybe he felt the need to attend to soul-lives.

Some say that one of the dis-eases of the western world/industrial growth society is that we do not attend to the needs of our souls, be that collectively or individually. Some commentators say that we have lost our souls, that we are technologically savvy but morally bankrupt. My work supports behavioural change programmes for men who are, or have been, abusive or violent to their women partners. We assist them in having relationships based on equality and non-abusive choices of behaviour. Men walk in through our door often hanging onto certainties about life, women, and the justifications for their behaviour. One strong theme is that they only acted to protect their children or in self-defence, even though their carefully constructed stories will usually contain a clue that this is not totally (or sometimes any of) the case. They walk in holding tightly and with both hands onto the illusion of being able to control all life, those close around them and situations, shit-scared that if they take a finger off for a second they will lose this and themselves with it. Some know somewhere, even if it's below their surface, that what they are doing isn't really working for them anymore. Sure, on one level it gets them what they want in an immediate and physical sense: obedience; nurturing; the last word; being at the centre of their world; being always in the right or a sense of order or even a literal way of ordering their world. But they know that something is misfiring or missing, even if they don't know what. On some level or for some of the time, usually after they've been violent or abusive in a way that is obvious to them, they feel bad for what they have done, even if they can't identify it as such just yet or hold onto the resolve never to do it again. Often the men who come to us are depressed, some to the point of suicidal thoughts. Some seek distraction from their "self" in drink or drugs or gambling or constant gam-

Some say that one of the dis-eases of the western world/industrial growth society is that we do not attend to the needs of our souls

ing or building a Walter Mitty[10] life for themselves. While not all men who abuse feel bad about it, they are probably the ones the programmes never see—at all or more than once or twice. But some get it—the ones who keep walking through the door and understand about the need to keep walking through the door bringing their destructive lives for us to break down and incubate.

They may not call it their soul but I have a sense that it is their internal life that is calling them to account, their emotions, their matter, their sense of honour. I would call this a soul. So maybe our process as workers is to do the carrion eaters' task. To gently break them down. To take the certainties and assumptions and take them apart. To bring the souls to Hel.

When we do and she takes them backwards, on their journey of growing younger, I think this is the process of unlearning. Most of what we offer to the men is exactly this. To let go of the false certainty of those damaging assumptions they've learnt and now hang onto and, if we're lucky, to trust a little more in the healthiness of a little chaos now and then (well, as much as a control freak can). We hope to get in between their ribs and poke around a bit. Shake the damaging and limiting beliefs. We try to help them unravel those assumptions, those false securities they are gripping onto. Trying to peel off the layers like those of an onion. To help them unlearn the destructive behaviours and take out that "toxic waste"[11] of their attitudes to

women and femaleness. We attempt to help them unlearn their beliefs in the myth of masculinity they have fallen for. We push a reset button in getting them to see that it is not only their view that matters and in setting up a (re)beginning to care for and about others. There is an aspect of this work that is like a less intense version of parenting, a re-parenting if you will. However, this is not to suggest that the cause of their behaviour is in bad parenting for a minute. Unless you consider parenting as a process done not just by parents but by society generally, too. It is more the process that we as workers do that I am referring to.

These men have trampled all over the boundaries others have tried to put in place. This always relates to those of their partners and children. It can also be in more general way and they will play out their resistance to the boundaries agreed with them by the workers and in a great many ways. We take on their appalling scapegoating of their partner. Usually she (and all women to a greater or lesser extent depending on the man) embodies everything they would hate about themselves or find problematic in a world where "male" attributes rule. Or much more accurately, in a society where some human attributes have been labelled "good" and "male" and others "bad" and "female".

We take their fingers, prized firmly on life, gripping their women, their soul, their children. We gently encourage them not to stranglehold others. Peel off the whitened knuckles and loosen the grip. Try to lead them to a place where they can start to find soul, diversity, emotional strength (rather than physical

We take their fingers, prized firmly on life, gripping their women, their soul, their children. We gently encourage them not to stranglehold others. Peel off the whitened knuckles and loosen the grip.

10   https://en.wikipedia.org/wiki/Walter_Mitty
11   Muddy Boots and Mistletoe, Incidental Druidry blog – "Cosmology and Compost."

strength with emotional brittleness). A place where they can just "be" and sit. Then let others "be" and be able to sit with that.

The process we, as workers, offer is to create spaces where we hold and "eat" their sins and, in doing so, to scapegoat ourselves for a while for them. But can we take on too much sin-food? I have certainly found myself in this situation. Stomach extended. Bloated from the taking on of too many meals. Eating too much sin. I have learnt that the trick is actually to try not to take on those person's sins as your own. Maybe sin-eaters never did. It was thought by others that they did. And certainly it is said by some that, if the sin-eater spoke, they spoke about absorbing the sins as their own. The very idea of eating sin, as we have it recorded, was to take in that person's sins into you with the food. But we don't know what the sin-eaters really made of this. This seems to me to be a very Christian-based thought, the idea of a Jesus-like sacrifice of one's self. There is also the irony of Jesus being outcast in his time but now revered, and how sin-eaters were outcast in their time. But if we hark back to an earlier time, there were other roles in a society that acted as a similar bridge between the living and the dead. Healer types, especially those we might refer to now as "shamans," although they might not have literally been called this back then.

When we believed in souls in this way, probably pre-Christian times, the shaman acted out of a societal belief that not all illnesses were physical in origin. A shaman, also usually living on the fringes of a society in some way, would be called upon to link the world of unseen and seen. S/he would reach into the other world(s), often through trance, and seek out answers from the spirits to bring back to heal those afflicted. This was less about taking on sins and more about a kind of channelling. Maybe, in our work with the men, that's what we need to learn to do. To reach into the mess of misogyny, violence, and abuse. To take those sins but to let them flow through us, using our skills to listen to the soul behind the immediate sins. To enter into the narrative of that man's life of deadness. To creep in, observe, and then seek out answers that work for that situation. To transform the illness of the soul, the hatred,

In some ways, there's a twisted logic to what abusive men do. It's really only the logical conclusion of the hatred of what we have labelled "feminine," embodied physically by women. They just take it a step further than other men do.

anger, self-righteousness, depression, shame, sense of failure. To do this by reaching in and offering solution. But for this work to mostly work through us. To pass through. Not to hang onto their sins as our own. To believe in the "possibility of possibilities,"[12] as one of my colleagues says, and which applies to the men in the groups as well as those of us running them. We become a kind of conduit and not a resting place. But we are still ourselves and we still put of our "selves" into the work. I do not mean a process with absence of our character or our personal humanity.

If we return to the image of the sin-eaters incubating the dead, we do not incubate them forever. Maybe this is what we offer. We offer to let parts of that person they were so sure about break down. We take the certainties about "how men should be" and the

12   John Petford.

assumptions of "how women are" and aim to disintegrate them. Dismantle them. Eat them. We take their sins: the absolute sense of right; the brittle displays of power; the manipulation. We put them in the acids of our stomach. It is a slow process but not really a gentle one. Stomach acids are very strong. But it shouldn't hurt. It is not destruction for its own sake. It is not a tearing down. We are "draining them of their powers"[13] because their powers are destructive. But our process is not solely one of conquering or defeating. It's not about taking into tiny pieces and leaving it like that. Whether you see this process as digestion or incubation, it is still a process of transformation. Even a process of alchemy perhaps. The process has to improve relationships. It has to have compassion. A re-birth. As a blog post on "Muddy Boots and Mistletoe" pointed out,

We as workers are like the body of a cauldron and in this way delineate the boundaries of the group. We hold the space in a way to enable the men to change, to meet Hel. But the heady mix in it—the brew, the potion, the concoction—that's where the change brews or melds.

> The destructive force is not just vanquished, in this tale; it is broken down, assimilated to the point that it enriches. The "irredeemable" detritus of a difficult life, or a life not well-lived, is broken down by these symbolic eaters of the dead to form the soil for new psychic growth. A long, painful process; one we don't discuss much, in our culture.[14]

To borrow ideas in the same post, things have to die, even in a small way, to make the conditions for renewal and life. You can't hang onto the idea of your partner as a useless mother and violent drunk and then treat her respectfully. The old ideas have to die to make room for new ones. They cannot both co-exist. Just as dead things put back in the land act as compost in order for other things to live. Just as cells in our bodies die off over time, so that new ones can replace them. "Death is more than just the end of life; it is the process by which life is possible."[15] As such, change is a form of death and death a form of change. I once blurted out in a group that, surely, change and death were the only certainties in life, to the accompanying sound of several men taking sharp intakes of breath and nearly clutching their chests. And this is so relevant for the groups we run, although there probably is a more subtle way to get this message across.

It isn't just the work of us, the sin-eaters. We take the men to Hel. And it probably is their idea of hell when they are first with us. All that sitting in a group with those men, those other ones that beat women up. Speaking about what they find intolerable in themselves or shameful or personal in front of a load of other men. Getting all touchy feely. Yuk. Who needs this?

It's no accident that Hel, the goddess to whom we take the men, is a woman. With most of the world fix-

13   Clarissa Pinkola Estes, *Women Who Run with the Wolves*
14   Muddy Boots and Mistletoe, Incidental Druidry blog – "Cosmology and Compost"
15   Muddy Boots and Mistletoe, Incidental Druidry blog – "Cosmology and Compost"

A BEAUTIFUL RESISTANCE

ated on one male god, where they are religious, and "male" values where they are not, we have forgotten the balance of the world. We have forgotten that once we honoured women as deity as well as men. The legacy we've inherited has considered men to be in charge—whether it be of country or home. We looked up to the sky and labelled it Go(o)d (male of course). We forgot that the Earth bore our weight and that women bore us. We got scared of death, emotion, and matter (the material nature of who we are). We looked to logic, reason, and the mind and worshipped these things at the expense of what we were now scared of. We labelled all the bad things as women, black people, or lesbians and gay men. As a society we valued only what was now labelled "male" and "white." What we feared in ourselves we scapegoated onto others and then we hated them and tried to keep them down. In some ways, there's a twisted logic to what abusive men do. It's really only the logical conclusion of the hatred of what we have labelled "feminine," embodied physically by women. They just take it a step further than other men do.

So, Hel, a woman goddess, is whom they need to face. They need to reconnect in a positive way to that which they think is "other," "evil," "feminine," or "scary." It's not as simple as getting-in-touch-with-your-feminine-side. I find that crassly underestimating what we (all) need to do. It is something more. It's not just accepting these things in themselves but in others. In women. In children. But it's also about giving up some of that power they wield over others. It's about knowing that being a man gives them a whole lot of privilege and that they have to stop themselves from exerting it and question what it is every day. Start the work of breaking it down. Get more humility. They can no longer let the predator in them roam freely but have to curtail its excesses. They have to capture their destructive thoughts before they lead to

He might get to rekindle a relationship. A second chance.

harmful behaviour and dismantle them. They have to learn how to eat their own sins. And before they get too big, unmanageable, and abusive.

We as workers are like the body of a cauldron and in this way delineate the boundaries of the group. We hold the space in a way to enable the men to change, to meet Hel. But the heady mix in it—the brew, the potion, the concoction—that's where the change brews or melds. Certain ingredients are picked that will go or "work" together, as when cooking a meal or brewing a potion. What is chosen is not random, although you may never be exactly sure how the dish will turn out. In the mix that is the brewing cauldron of the group, the ingredients may change form. Then, over time, the ingredients make something different. Something that mixes together as a whole, not just different things randomly introduced, that remain. The creation becomes more than the sum of its ingredients. Just as the men's stories become more than haphazardly assigned parts. If it works, the process sees the creation of something new that works, that hangs together, that is coherent. We might see that keeping everything the same or static is now less important. We might see men drop the brittle carapace or subtle, or not so subtle, stereotypical views of women, mixed with their own sense of right, or with the blueprint for destruction of self and others that is the dominant form of masculinity (to adapt a phrase by Utah Phillips).

No food is without nourishment, except most fast food, but this process is slow cooking. Most group facilitators I speak to seem to get an amount of personal growth in these cauldrons of transformation. In this case it might be insight into human emotions or, at worst, a lesson in how not to behave in relating to others. A way to check ourselves. It may be a lesson in how to try to drop the human need to control. And a reminder of the consequences of doing this. Or the hopelessness and frustration and damage of acting this way in the world. We can all take the nourishment we need.

But, when we eat, we don't take all the stuff from the food on board. We take what we need for energy. We digest it and then "waste" some. If we didn't we'd get bloated and just fatter and fatter. Shitting what we don't require is part of a necessary digesting process. So maybe that's the key to working with these men. Don't let the assumptions stick. Don't let the "shit" they say stick to your insides. There are no nutrients there. Especially as a woman facilitator. We also need to let go of the men's resentment, the misogyny, the assumptions about women. It's not ours to own—we don't need to hold into it. There's so much about letting go in this work, all through the programme and, most obviously, at the end of it. If you are pregnant, you have to give birth at some point. You can't hang onto the baby inside you forever. The baby has our fingerprints on her/him but it becomes its own being. We let her/him go. First out of our bodies, then out of our homes. Eighteen years later or so, if you're lucky(!). Just as we let the men go after the programme. And of course we'll be there for support if they need us, but not every week once they leave home and we'll no longer be doing their dirty washing. And we have to let go too. As much as I'd like some of them on a group for the rest of their lives, I have to let go. It is impractical and impossible not to.

Then, at the end of the programme, the men we see have hopefully travelled backwards enough to be re-born. In this case, he is unlikely to be a new person, that would be an unrealistic goal, but he may feel lighter, younger, no longer depressed. He may feel that his formerly broken parts are on the way to becoming integrated. He may get a renewed chance at life, though. He might get to rekindle a relationship. A second chance. Maybe make amends. He may start the road to being a safer partner, a better father. Even if the couple is no longer together, he may understand the need for respectful co-parenting and be able to be a good dad rather than someone who just "has" to see "his" children. He may see how he needs to behave with future partners, and lose the cynical view of all women and how-bad-we-all-are. He lets others breathe around him, gives them space to be themselves, takes steps back when he needs to rather than wading in with his opinion or his might. When the men get it, they also realise that this is not the end for them but the beginning of a long journey and one that takes constant effort. For us, our eating of their sin is over. We've encouraged them to grow their positives and curtail their negatives. But we haven't taken everything away, we've left that person intact hoping to have changed some of their abusive behaviours. We have hopefully inspired them, not to tell a different story, but to tell their story differently.

NINA GEORGE

Nina George lives in Lancashire in North West England and is a social activist, working on tackling gender-based violence across Europe. She agitates for revolution whenever she can (this may be the reason she is never employee of the month!). She blogs intermittently at https:// breathingfireintowhoweare.wordpress.com/

The Druidry of Mapping

Nimue Brown

A map, I think is in essence an image of our relationship with the land. Any given physical map will present itself to you as an accurate portrayal of that which is mapped, but it's never really that simple. A map involves sets of choices about what to include or exclude. Those choices express values and priorities, beliefs about importance and irrelevance. As a consequence, most of the maps a western person encounters are road maps. I am less certain about other parts of the world. Detailed mapping tends to be urban, and will focus on human constructs. Get into more rural areas and maps are about footpaths, field boundaries, and other indications of human ownership. Where we are allowed to go, and where is forbidden to us, is mapped. Where the deer go is not.

Map making is deeply tied to the idea of land ownership, and maps are key in proving that most ludicrous of human notions—who owns which piece of ground. Mapping goes with naming, and naming is also a form of possession and colonisation. Previous cultures are literally wiped off the map, to be replaced by the names, terms, and priorities of the map maker, and the money behind the map maker.

LEFT SACRED

On a normal road map, wild places are blanks, or empty green spaces. If, as many people do, you replace the road map with sat nav, you won't even see that there are any green bits most of the time. The map the sat nav holds within it represents the world of road and post code. Granted, there are sat navs for walkers, and I've never used them. I like to see the map for myself, and the prejudices inherent in the map, as I'm going along. At least that way I'll get some clues as to what I might be missing.

Some human maps are so abstract, so obsessed with the human that they bear no resemblance to the physical world at all. I am thinking about the maps of the London Underground as I type this—beautiful, tidy things that drive me mad because my little brain cannot hold any relationship between this map and my physical experience of places. Such maps are not means to connect us to the land, but to connect us to our work places and shopping opportunities. The land is of no importance in the world of the tube, it seems.

The Druidry of mapping is something I've been thinking about for a while now. People living in traditional cultures around the world are renowned for their ability to carry internal maps. These can take all kinds of forms, including song and story, and they enable a person to know and navigate through wild environments. Most of us do not have these inner maps. One of the things that conventional map making has done to western people is to discourage this. I think sat nav is even worse, making people ignorant of where they are and where everything else is in relationship to them.

Making an inner map is a process of developing real relationship with the land. A map built from experience, from knowing a place by taking your body out into it, may not be easily expressed and will never fit tidily on a page. It's not just a map through a place that you get with inner map making, but a map of time as well. Places change through the seasons. Routes open up or close depending on the conditions. Views appear and disappear with the leaves. An inner map holds the cyclical nature of the place, and the linear changes over time. It holds the shape of the land and the stories of our being in it.

The beginning of inner map making is to work out what kinds of maps you already have. This can be assessed by contemplating your sense of place, writing about it, trying to draw it or any other means you can think of to make what you hold unconsciously visible to you. Looking at standard maps can help a person work out where their own inner map deviates from what's on the page. Then the questions arise as to what we might want to map. What kinds of features need to take priority? Maps teach us that we can't have everything, that we must pick what to include and what to leave out. A perfect map of a place would of course have to be the same size of the place itself, and thus cannot be used. What do we leave out in order to change the scale? What do we need to navigate? What do we need to understand? Which details can we afford to be less focused on?

The map a person makes to traverse terrain is not the same as a map you make to hunt or forage in it, and that's not the same as a leisure map, or a map of sacred places. The woods person's map is very different from the stone worker's map. Maps

> Map making is deeply tied to the idea of land ownership, and maps are key in proving that most ludicrous of human notions—who owns which piece of ground.

of fishing and swimming are different again. For those who can get airborne, a whole other approach to mapping must be required.

Then, as poets we may think of the things that cannot be mapped. Cartography of the clouds and of snow drifts, the geography of autumn leaf drifts and the ripples in streams. We can look at the stars for maps as our ancestors have done, but we can only guess at the stories swans teach their young in order to use those same star maps for orientation in long migrations. What kind of maps do frogs and salmon use to get back to the places of their birth? How do moles map their underground journeys? What kinds of maps does an arctic tern make? Or a whale?

A big part of the problem with human map making is that it is so relentlessly human-centric. It reveals all of our prejudices and assumptions, and our destructive, consumption-led ways of being. There aren't any stories in our road maps, not even the stories of the people who lived and died building the roads. At best all we can do is infer stories from place names. Conventional maps hold in them the belief that everything can be measured, known, and laid out on paper for easy human scrutiny. There are no maps of the way moonlight touches the ground in a wood, and there are no maps of places that might be doorways into faerie. But just now and then, there are tiny patches of landscape that defy the map makers, even in relentlessly known rural England. I have found places where the regular maps and signposts don't quite work, and where there is, as a consequence, a hint of wonder to be found.

Druidic map making is an act of unmaking the maps in our heads that tie us to money, ownership, road, and boundary. Take those things out of our sense of place, and what remains? Something unknown. Something potentially wild and unfamiliar. The uncharted path towards personal re-enchantment.

NIMUE BROWN

Nimue Brown writes blogs, novels, graphic novels and non-fic titles on Paganism. She walks, ponders, and obsesses her way around the hills and valleys of Stroud, Gloucestershire and has recently discovered the possibilities of making maps of imaginary places. Find her at www. druidlife.wordpress.com

THE REAWAKENING OF TRIBAL CONSCIOUSNESS: THE SPREAD OF ECOLOGICAL WISDOM AND CONFRONTING THE ARTIFICE OF CAPITALISM

William Hawes

"When we learn to come together we are whole
when we learn to recognize the enemy
we will know what we need to know
to learn to come together
to learn to weave and mend."
—Anne Cameron, Daughters of Copper Woman

"I am the guardian of life
and death

all my children come back to me

I call you
conjure you
hide you in my breast
you nourish me with your bones

and live again.
I am your Mother Earth

your dark Mother Earth.

If you insist on destroying me

 you will destroy yourselves.

Wake up
my children

listen to my cry."
—Claribel Alegría, "Gaia's Cry"

Recent world events are playing out a drama unseen since the mid-17th century. When the Treaty of Westphalia was signed in 1648, European borders were drawn so that sovereign states would establish the sole rule of law within their own respective territories. Today, transnational capitalism, huge waves of immigrants from war-torn and poverty-stricken regions, instant globe-spanning internet communication, and the threat of fundamentalist terrorism are dissolving borders at a rapid pace. In its wake, the notions of duty, respect for environmental rights, citizenship, and nations are being reformed to shape this rapidly forming interconnected global culture. Leaders of modern nation-states are proving less and less adept at handling crises and managing world affairs: they turn to various technocrats within the maze of various government ministries, powerful businesspeople whose lobbyists write the laws for the legislature, non-profits and NGOs who carry out needed health and infrastructure projects, and community leaders from civil society who are able to wade through ethnic and tribal antagonisms with ease.

LEFT SACRED

As nations falter due to weak links of shared identity between citizens, new ecologically and culturally conscious groups of people are linking together, as globe-spanning tribes based on tradition, ritual, spirituality, reciprocity, and love of the environment are gathering to create the most important movement of the 21st century. As refugees from the Middle East flee warfare, as Latin Americans leave their homelands due to little or no job security, and as highly educated East and South Asians emigrate to pursue advanced careers in engineering, science, and more, global tribes are forming that transcend the modern nation-state. Millions of people now have dual citizenships, and conflicting allegiances between their nation of birth and their new homes.

The Western state is now collapsing under the weight of its own bloated bureaucracies, its satiated, anesthetized, and myopic views of politics, and its inability, its unwillingness, to confront the environmental destruction and social ennui endemic to capitalism. The predatory nature of the state, its capacity for resource extraction and organized violence, is becoming all too clear for globally oriented people, those who adhere to a one-world philosophy and a desire to eliminate borders. Many young people are beginning to consider themselves as world citizens, or at least as member of larger regions, just as people in the EU refer to European citizenship and the European community. In the Islamic world, a similar concept has been used for centuries: Muslims are members of the ummah, the collective community of believers in Islam.

The Vision of Global Tribes

These questions surrounding transnational violence, religious fundamentalism, world citizenship, and social backgrounds are explored in depth in Amin Maaolouf's *In the Name of Identity: Violence and the Need to Belong*. Maalouf traces his personal background, explains why having numerous tribal and ethnic allegiances does not inevitably have to lead to conflict, how modern Western nations react to "the other," and most importantly, explains his notion of global tribes. He asserts that in contemporary life we have reached "The Age of Global Tribes," a new era in which a patchwork of shifting ethnic, religious, and tribal allegiances compete with nation-states for glory, the need for social identity, and power.

Maalouf focuses on the Arab world, due to his dual French-Lebanese background. For Maalouf, fundamentalist Islamism gives disaffected individuals in undemocratic, dictatorial regimes a stable identity, despite the possibility of fomenting hatred and nihilism that fundamentalism can lead to. The corollaries in Western society would be people like Timothy McVeigh, Anders Breivik, the Unabomber, and the odd racist or militia group that advocates violence. While it would be tidy to lay all the blame on a nihilistic outlook, on the death drive (Freud's Thanatos), this seems an oversimplification. For the young, well-ed-

> Today, transnational capitalism, huge waves of immigrants from war-torn and poverty-stricken regions, instant globe-spanning internet communication, and the threat of fundamentalist terrorism are dissolving borders at a rapid pace.

A BEAUTIFUL RESISTANCE

ucated, and politically-oriented men in Arab nations, but those not rich enough to emigrate to the West or enjoy the simulacra consumer "paradise" that Arab nations try to copy, there are few options for social belonging. Fifty years ago, Marxist groups would have provided an outlet for social belonging; thirty years ago, the examples of Nasser, Sadat, and Khomeini led youths towards pan-Arab or nationalist organizations. Today, with the failure of both, and the covert support of the Gulf monarchies and their Western backers for jihadi terror, Islamist groups provide the need for social belonging in a very small percentage of young Arabs. Maalouf explains: "In [Islamism] they find satisfaction for their need for identity, for affiliation to a group, for spirituality, for a simple interpretation of too-complex realities and for action and revolt."[16]

The need to find affiliation for young people is partly due to the continued pattern of the modern nation-state de-legitimizing itself: by promoting structural racism, by allowing its laws and court systems to uphold neoliberal privatizations against the will of the people, by using "anti-terrorist" laws and emergency powers to murder wantonly around the globe, and by keeping domestic citizens in a state of panic and submission. With government officials more beholden to transnational corporations than national sovereignty and public welfare, citizens no longer have a basic

16   Amin Maalouf. *In the Name of Identity: Violence and the Need to Belong.* p. 90. Penguin Books, New York, 2000.

sense of security, community, and camaraderie.

When youth no longer feel a sense of pride or even respect for their homelands, and no communal or familial groups can provide a healthy sense of identity, it is not unusual for disaffection, religious extremism, and nihilism to grow, filling the void. This can be seen as a distinctly modern form of malaise, and can occur just as easily in an authoritarian Middle Eastern nation as in a "modern" Western country, where we have been inculcated since birth that consumerism and the constant need to get ahead in the corporate world are our only outlets for creative expression and productive work.

The construct of the nation-state, and its right to exist, has been delegitimized by the failed ideologies of Marxism in Eastern Europe, Maoism in East Asia, permanent ethnic conflict in Africa, dictatorships in the Mideast, unregulated capitalism in North America and Western Europe, and the machismo populism prevalent in parts of Latin America. Each ideology essentially provided "cover" for authoritarian, Machiavellian laws to come into being; for the state monopolization of violence; and for wealth to be funneled upwards from the commons to the ruling class. Now that the legalized brutality and robbery is plain for all to see, via the rise of the internet and alternative media, there can be no doubt that nations will be forced to cede power to local, state, and autonomously-governed regions, in an unfolding of governmental

> When youth no longer feel a sense of pride or even respect for their homelands, and no communal or familial groups can provide a healthy sense of identity, it is not unusual for disaffection, religious extremism, and nihilism to grow, filling the void.

decentralization which will take decades, if not centuries, to blossom worldwide.

Thus it is no surprise to Maalouf and others that religion is what groups will fall back on in the modern era of crony capitalism and ecological disaster. Maalouf's solution is language: if we all learn to adopt three (or more) languages, cultural differences and tensions will relax, and a true world community where religious belief no longer coincides with group violence can flourish.

Neo-Tribal Consciousness and Organization

What is missing from Maalouf's analysis is the organization of this future society. For author Daniel Quinn, it is the tribe that will become the backbone of our emerging culture. He explores these ideals in his book *Beyond Civilization,* where he calls for a "New Tribal Revolution." And in many ways the neo-tribal group seems the best option: tribes which share the work and share the profit of collective endeavors will inevitably have much less inequality and are likely be much more peaceful. As Quinn explains:

> Tribal life is not in fact perfect, idyllic, noble, or wonderful, but wherever it's found intact, it's found to be working well—as well as the life of lizards, racoons, geese, or beetles—with the result that the members of the tribe are not generally enraged, rebellious, desperate, stressed-out borderline psychotics being torn apart by crime, hatred, and violence. What anthropologists find is that tribal peoples, far from being nobler, sweeter, or wiser than us, are as capable as we are of being mean, unkind, short-sighted, selfish, insensitive, stubborn, and short-tempered. The tribal life doesn't turn people into saints; it enables ordinary people to make a living together with a minimum of stress year after year, generation after generation.[17]

A new form of tribe is emerging, not the suffocating,

17   Daniel Quinn. *Beyond Civilization: Humanity's Next Great Adventure.* p. 61. Three Rivers Press, New York, 1999.

tyrannical, stereotypical, monotype tribe of the kind we read about in school history books: new groups where tradition does not dictate every action of the individual, where individuals feel free to express their spirituality without the needed to conform to a group religion. An egalitarian tribe, where merit matters, not rigid hierarchy or nepotism. Most importantly, neo-tribal wisdom accepts the idea that ecocentrism is central: the idea that humanity is not center stage in a drama located on planet Earth; the idea that we are all part of a cosmic web, a sacred hoop in Native American terms; that the environment does not derive its worth from human value, but has innate value and should be protected from short-term exploitation. For Quinn, the new tribal revolution is distinctly postmodern: it signifies the end of meta-narratives, the end of the idea that, in his words "There is only one right way to live": the end of the superficial, spiritually myopic way of the modern techno-capitalist state.

The Delusion of Left vs. Right

Viewing the world from the holistic, ecocentrist way, the futile arguments over liberal versus conservative beliefs are unmasked for what they are: a distraction, a carnival. The antagonism of Liberal/Conservative is thus a collective hallucination designed by elites to divide and conquer the people, as well as destroy ecosystems and pillage resources. Capitalist and Marxist-Leninist communist societies controlled by oligarchies have both ravaged environments immensely, and both have had industrial growth at the heart of their belief system. They both constitute, for author Jonathon Porritt, a super-ideology: industrialism. Here's Porritt:

> "[Capitalism and Communism] are dedicated to industrial growth, to the expansion of the means of production, to a materialist ethic as the best means of meeting people's needs, and to unimpeded technological development. Both rely on increasing centralization and large-scale bureaucratic control and coordination. From a viewpoint of narrow

scientific rationalism, both insist that the planet is there to be conquered, that big is self-evidently beautiful, and that what cannot be measured is of no importance."[18]

The most pertinent politics to our collective survival is how the human race uses and protects its lands and waters for the betterment of our own societies, our future children, and our fellow plant and animal species. How we can in small groups, clans, tribes, and perhaps even bioregional city-states grow enough food, collect enough clean water, gather materials for shelter, use appropriately scaled technology, and foster a vibrant culture among peaceable citizens. This philosophy goes by many names: sustainability, deep ecology, ecocentrism, etc. Indigenous cultures have been practicing these skills for millennia, passing on oral traditions and ecological and agricultural knowledge so detailed it would make the Library of Congress look insignificant in comparison. Much of this knowledge and ancient wisdom has been lost to the sands of time, victim of the uprooting of cultures because of colonial wars, epidemic diseases, the techno-reductionism of modern health and science, capitalism, and Christianity's missionary engulfment over entire continents, and more.

Ideas surrounding ecocentric politics, liberty, and democracy are being questioned from new radical perspectives, although Western media blacks out massive progress: in Ecuador and Bolivia, the socialist parties

> Maalouf's solution is language: if we all learn to adopt three (or more) languages, cultural differences and tensions will relax, and a true world community where religious belief no longer coincides with group violence can flourish.

in power are immensely raising standards of living and education, while improving rights for the environment and indigenous groups. In Spain, Podemos' combination of direct and digital democracy, and its citizen circles used to debate local and municipal issues are redefining European politics. In the state of Chiapas, Mexico, Zapatistas led by the EZLN group have been busy for the past twenty-one years opening schools and hospitals, redistributing farmland for struggling farmers, saving diverse rainforests from logging and grazing, and imparting deep ecological values to their youth. Also, the EZLN are committed to passing on their own traditional Mayan culture within a framework of egalitarian deals, communalism, and socialist beliefs, distancing themselves from the whirlwind of colonial capitalism that lords over most of North, Central, and South America.

What is also interesting is that many of these new perspectives and leaders are not committed to the ossifying processes that soon results from traditional political parties and the levels of bureaucracy that ensue. Groups like Bolivia's MAS party and the EZLN have begun to embody the ideal of direct, grassroots participatory democracy. This is because it is only the people of a nation, its citizens, and not the faceless multinational corporations and their political figureheads, who are able to understand that inequality, injustice, and environmental degradation are a direct result of capitalism-induced poverty, resource consumption, a loss of choices in the public sphere, and lack of regulations and care for the Earth.

18   As quoted in Andrew Dobson. *Green Political Thought* (4th ed.). Routledge, New York, 2007.

The Paradox of Modern Education: Liberation versus Indoctrination

Today, modern Western education systems are playing a dual and contradictory role: edifying our youth and steeping them in critical ecological knowledge and value systems, while at the same time indoctrinating them into a corporate and conformist lifestyle by teaching them to obey and buy the products of the multinational companies pillaging the Earth.

Possibly the most intelligent tract concerning modern-day mindlessness when it comes to education is Paul Goodman's devastatingly accurate *Growing Up Absurd*. Written back in 1960, Goodman torched the official out-of-touch education system, and laments the disaffected youths who feel excluded from capitalism and the anomie that emerges. Still immensely relevant today, Goodman explains the sheer naivety and blind spots of western pedagogical methods:

> Social scientists ... have begun to think that "social animal" means "harmoniously belonging." They do not like to think that fighting and dissenting are proper social functions, nor that rebelling or initiating fundamental change is a social function. Rather, if something does not run smoothly, they say it has been improperly socialized; there has been a failure in communication. ... But perhaps there has not been a failure in communication. Perhaps the social message has been communicated clearly...and is unacceptable. ... We must ask the question, "Is the harmonious organization to which the young are inadequately socialized perhaps against human nature, or not worthy of human nature, and therefore there is difficulty in growing up?[19]

19   Paul Goodman. *Growing Up Absurd.* p. 10-11. Vintage, New York, 1960.

A BEAUTIFUL RESISTANCE

Goodman's analysis of juvenile delinquency, the lack of hope and prospects for young people, as well as his treatment on many issues including the structural racism of the prison system, and the missed revolutions in modern society are devastatingly accurate today. Education which focuses on world cultures, equality, indigenous beliefs, sustainability, and love of nature for its own sake and not human instrumental needs, teachings outside the Eurocentric worldview, will foster an ecocentric outlook, and progress then can be made towards a peaceful world community.

The Anatomy of Power

The modern nation-state faces a series of contradictions, not just in health, agriculture, and education. It simply is becoming more impotent at solving problems in mass society due to layers of bureaucracy, inflation of the currency which makes every social service more expensive to implement, the hollowing out of community services due to privatizations, etc. And problems of an interconnected, interdependent, globalized world lie outside the reach of the state. In Daniel Bell's words, nations "have become too small to solve big problems, too big to solve small problems."

States in the 21st century are most likely to function and thrive by governing horizontally: with many connections between workers unions, local politicians, civic groups, environmental non-profits, etc. In this way, local production takes precedence over mass-manufactured goods from China and places halfway across the world, lowering greenhouse emissions. Thus practices of bioregionalism are employed, and what experts might call the "topology of power relations" is changed to include environmental concerns and forms of eco-cultural restoration. Culture can then recreate itself around annual agricultural and ethically-responsible means of production, and recreate its connection to time and space: rather than continuing exclusively under the atomized Gregorian time system and borders imposed by conniving politicians, our world culture can work, play, and sink into the ever-present moment, what the Aborigines call the Dreaming.

If power is already beginning to be dispersed tribally, and through bioregional processes, are there any examples we can point to? Certainly, in the West, the case of the breakup of Yugoslavia, referendums in Quebec and Scotland, and the fight for a referendum in Catalonia all qualify as sub-national tribal entities reasserting their right to self-rule. Further, in the region of the former Soviet Union, the cases of Abkhazia, South Ossetia, East Ukraine, and Crimea, while they are often vilified as a form of ethno-nationalist fascism originating in the Kremlin, are undoubtedly due to the tribal allegiances shared between these fragile mini-states and the Russian motherland.

There are even wannabe theorists in the US who claim to have identified the tribal identities in the USA, such as Colin Woodward and Joel Garreau.. Both authors appear to be older, white, privileged, and seemingly unaware that US culture is very homogenous, and perhaps didn't consider that there are vastly fewer cultural differences between New York and California, a 3,000 mile trek, than, say, the short hop between Brussels and Amsterdam.

For example, in 1830, Belgium split apart from the Netherlands due to myriad social, economic, and ethnic differences, despite large cultural commonalities and a huge trading economy. In the Netherlands, Dutch is spoken almost universally; Frisian, a Germanic language, also is used, and Protestantism is the dominant form of Christianity. In Belgium, Dutch is the language of the north (Flanders), while French is spoken in the south (Wallonia) and Catholicism is the most popular religion in the country. The US has no such comparable divide today: the last time one occurred, of course, resulted in the Civil War.

Further Garreau does not even have any territory set aside for the First Nations, the Native Americans whose ancestors lived here for millennia, while Woodward only includes land in Northern Canada and Alaska for First Nation status, apparently oblivious to the 333 federally recognized Indian Nations in the US that are not in Alaska.

Badiou's Rebirth of History

The most striking examples of tribal, sub-national, mass movement intuitive wisdom towards rebellion and revolution against corrupt nations can be found in the 2011 Arab Spring, the Occupy Wall Street movement, and Spain's Indignados. In all three instances, it was an activist minority who ignited popular dissatisfaction against corrupt regimes: in the West, oligarchic capitalism; in the Arab world, the figure of the Western-backed strongman, the dictator. For philosopher Alain Badiou, each of these dedicated protests represents a historical riot: an attempt to portray a political Truth to the world. Further, these acts showed that they represented the true will of the people, in the most general and universal terms: even though they accounted for a tiny minority, mainstream media regularly referred to Egyptian protesters at Tahrir Square as democratic, as representing the will of the people.

Of course, in the Middle East and North Africa the Arab Spring was about much more than democracy in any representative, parliamentarian sense: besides throwing out dictators like Mubarak and Ben Ali, social justice, dignity, equality, and freedom from Western hegemony were among key issues. The state should not have total power to determine law, taxes, industrial organization: civil society and direct democracy has a role to play as well. For the state, this is non-negotiable. As Badiou puts it:

> A massive popular event creates a destatification of the issue of what is possible. In general, and especially in recent decades, the state has arrogated to itself the right to say what is possible in the political order and what is not. It is thus possible to "humanize" capitalism and "develop" democracy. But to construct a productive, institutional social order normed by equality and genuine popular command—that is completely impossible, a fatal utopia.[20]

To Badiou, the instincts of these protesters are correct in the sense that they tend towards universality: the values expressed (freedom, justice, forcing dictators to step down, etc.) not only apply to the nations involved, but are political truths the whole world must accept. This marks our age as an interregnum, or as Badiou says, an intervallic period, a stage between crony capitalism and a possible future world order of justice and egalitarianism. History is being born again out of the Thatcher-Reagan period of hyper-capitalism from approximately 1980-2011, where greed was good, deregulation and privatization ruled, and the World Bank and IMF plundered the developing nations. The rise of civil society and grassroots democracy will lead to the withering away of the state, to Communism, in Badiou's mind. For other theorists, ecologism is the preferred term to refer to the future era of politics; for others, bioregionalism, or environmental democracy.

20 http://ouleft.org/wp-content/uploads/Badiou-Riots-and-Uprisings.pdf p. 94.

This marks our age as an interregnum, or as Badiou says, an intervallic period, a stage between crony capitalism and a possible future world order of justice and egalitarianism.

Despite the differences in the symbolic nomenclature, in ideology, there are key similarities between theorists of leftist political thought, and though they are hesitant to use terminology of the tribe, their principles often align with indigenous groups: smaller organizations of well-integrated peoples living and working together, with forms of consensus, direct democracy, horizontal civic groups, and yes, even tribal and religious elders who will uphold essential traditions, rituals, and spirituality necessary for group survival and cultural enrichment.

Lessons from Anthropology

For cultural anthropologist John H. Bodley, there are three cultural worlds: the tribal, the imperial, and the commercial. Most 21st century states are commercial states, dependent on industrialization, fossil fuels, high technology, global markets and cities, and representative government. Yet as he points out, "Commercialization co-opts both humanization and politicization processes to promote economic growth and the accumulation of financial capital."[21] Political "elites" agree, although they use vague and convoluted arguments, threats, rhetoric, and would demur from ever saying so in such a blunt manner. For instance, the humanism of the 1948 UN Universal Declaration of Human Rights is now seen as idealistic and unworkable by most "modern" Western states. The politicization process begun in the Enlightenment now begins and ends with liberal democracy, which today only buys time for authoritarian capitalism and the oligarchy that funnels money to the one-percent and their multinationals.

The commercial (liberal) arguments that restricting personal freedoms and thinning out the social commons are necessary for civilization are simply cases of falling for one's own propaganda. The most glaring and infamous recent example being Fukuyama's *The End of History*, in which he posits free-market capitalism, liberal democracy, and globalization marked the end of world conflict, the rising of standards of living globally, and that liberal capitalism was the last and greatest socioeconomic ideology. These are "Delusions of Progress" according to Bodley. Bodley rejects the materialist technological, epidemiological, and geographical reasons for Eurocentric dominance (Jared Diamond's *Guns, Germs, and Steel* argument) in the imperial and commercial worlds, and for him:

> The fate of humanity is determined by three variables...the scale at which people organize their sociocultural systems...how people control social power...and their deceptive use of culture to control perception.[22]

In the imperial states of the 16th century through the commercial states in the 21st, the Westphalian states meet all three criteria for domination of weaker tribes and small nations. Recall the huge organizational scale of Spanish, Dutch, British, and French empires; the figure of the leader, replaced by rulers and later parliaments who demand tribute in the form of taxes to control social power; and the use of ideology and black propaganda for nefarious purposes (consider the hypocritical and murderous rhetoric of Manifest Destiny, the Monroe Doctrine, Bush's "War on Terror," Adam Smith's "invisible hand." etc.).

The Global System, Political Ecologism, and Their Limits

Global institutions like the UN, World Trade Organization, the EU, and their associated NGOs are simply not equipped to handle the flood of crises that scientific and social experts are predicting. And the nation-state will not be ready to handle issues when the floodgates open either. There are calls from a few (mostly ignored) expert theorists to begin planning for what they call the Eco-state, or the Green State,[23] which will delegate responsibility of the bottom-up

---

21   John H. Bodley. *Cultural Anthropology: Tribes, States, and the Global System*. (5th ed.) p. 17. Altamira, Plymouth, 2011.

22   ibid. p. 19.

23   Robyn Eckersely. *The Green State*. MIT Press, Cambridge, MA, 2004.

duties of social welfare and assign them to civil society, non-profits, and grassroots citizen groups; and the top-down, streamlined hierarchy of government responsible for natural disasters, tax collection, defense, and integrating trade within the global architecture. Green political ecologism does impart an especially important lesson, one that tribal societies understand implicitly: expanding the moral community to provide political protection for the rights of future human generations, non-human life forms, and the biosphere as a whole.

Political elites are not interested in imparting these deep ecological values: the elites instead appeal to the darkest, craven, lowest-common-denominator voter who refuses to consider lowering their habits of consumption. Everything could be changed by sharply limiting what we buy, lowering meat and especially beef consumption, rationing fossil fuel use, etc.: quality of life would vastly improve, average lifespan would increase, the arts would be rejuvenated, and morally responsible technology would develop.

As long as elites are bought by lobbyists pushing corporate agendas, and electorates are unwilling to see that the "standard of living" does not equate with the amount of things one owns, the green state and the interlocking global framework it requires seems far off. Perhaps the late 21st or the 22nd century will provide the state system needed for ecological stability and interdependence. For now, the smaller scale of the tribe will have to suffice.

Tribal Seeds: Reproducing Culture from Time Immemorial

While great philosophers like Badiou extol communism, and green theorists such as Dobson and Eckersely promote ecological politics, the annals of history and examples of indigenous tribes today can provide a model for the future. As Bodley shows, it is the tribal world that knows how to reproduce culture. Small-scale tribes are less likely to use organized violence as a tool for coercive and deadly clashes with rival nations, and much more likely to use sustainable farming and technology. A sharing and bartering society, with organic, biodynamic agricultural practices nourishing people materially and spiritually, would go a long way towards healing the open wounds of our mother Earth and the ethnic and sectarian tensions plaguing most nations. Rather than keeping food, housing, and material and intellectual property under lock and key, a culture of abundance would allow unparalleled access to health, education, and scale-appropriate technology.

All the while, transnational notions of identity allow numerous chances for the cross-fertilization of

> As mass movements rally for social justice and direct democracy, the idea of what a tribal nation can be will spark a change in the public, and the struggle for liberation from suicidal capitalism and respect for universal human rights dissolve people's delusions that a tribe must be xenophobic and antidemocratic.

sub-national groups and tribes. Civic engagement is slowly regaining strength as citizens want to expand communal gardening and agricultural practices, energy-efficient housing and irrigation, and renewable energy projects. As mass movements rally for social justice and direct democracy, the idea of what a tribal nation can be will spark a change in the public, and the struggle for liberation from suicidal capitalism and respect for universal human rights dissolve people's delusions that a tribe must be xenophobic and anti-democratic.

Tribal society can be insular when it comes to one issue, however: the idea of reproducing culture. Certain rituals and rites of passage remain a closely guarded secret for many tribes, because of their profound mystical and spiritual implications. Shamans and chieftains in indigenous society are trained their whole lives to guide and groom the next generation: there are risks involved when passing through stages of life and traveling through spiritual realms. Similarly, the industrialized nations face similar risks today, which can only be solved by a tribe, a village, a community. We must invent ways where we can initiate youths and adolescents, mothers and fathers, so that they can develop harmoniously within the social fabric. We must confront the ennui and malaise that the consumer culture has spawned. And hopefully, then we can learn the holy, sacred secrets to reproducing and recreating ecosystems and cultures worth passing on to the next generation.

WILLIAM HAWES

William Hawes is a husband, father, and writer. His work can be found online at the websites Global Research, Counterpunch, Dissident Voice, Countercurrents, Dissident Voice, and The World Financial Review. You can find his ebook, Planetary Vision: Essays on Freedom and Empire, on Amazon.

LIA HUNTER

Lia Hunter is an awenydd, OBOD bard, mother, naturalist, and anthropology student from the U.S. Mountain West. She strives to be a good ancestor and to tend the garden of culture so that harmful weed-memes will stop choking out the humans and society we could be.

BELL UNRUNG

Lia Hunter

I've discovered a thick bell
inside of me
that elegiac poetry rings
a terribly deep booming
knell

It has always been there, I can tell
but I had forgotten
I think it is in all of us
a human ache, a fathomless
well

Being dead while alive mutes its swell
wraps the bell in fog and distance
and it must be one of the Mysteries
that you have to be alive to feel
its peal

that resounding shake of loss in your core
that throws all semblance to hell

Depression... could its fog be protection?
from all we have lost and are losing?
But a quelling that keeps us dead
In the face of death
And life

A society that does not realize it is in mourning
that grief is appropriate
that an elegy is going unsung
yet still death is
come

THE IMPURE OBJECT OF THE LEFT SACRED

Finnchuill

The levels of impurities in a material are generally defined in relative terms. Standards have been established by various organizations that attempt to define the permitted levels of various impurities in a manufactured product. Strictly speaking, then a material's level of purity can only be stated as being more or less pure than some other material.

No matter what method is used, it is usually impossible to separate an impurity completely from a material. The reason that it is impossible to remove impurities completely is of thermodynamic nature and is predicted by the second law of thermodynamics. Removing impurities completely means reducing the entropy of the system to zero. This would require an infinite amount of work and energy as predicted by the second law of thermodynamics. What technicians can do is to increase the purity of a material to as near 100% as possible or economically feasible.

—Wikipedia

Purity is searched for in the laboratory, in sober separations of matter from matter; in the demarcations of laws; in certain religious practices. The removal of impurities is an elaborate quest of separations, a ceaseless maintenance of identity, a structuring of language and matter. Yet the transgression of limits of the pure is one of the great powers of the sacred, the impure left sacred which is full of potential for liberatory force. The left hand sacred, dangerous and impure, was integral to past Pagan/polytheist practices, and needs to be again.

The western imagination is much influenced in its thoughts on purity and impurity by the Book of Leviticus. Mary Douglas, an American anthropologist, analyzed purity and defilement through an analysis of that Biblical work in her 1966 book, *Purity and Danger*. She wrote, "Defilement is never an isolated event. It cannot occur except in view of a systematic ordering of ideas." At the beginning of her investigation, she asked why would the hyrax, the hare, and the camel be impure, but the frog and gazelle clean and the hippopotamus not, and some locusts but not all?

While the abominations of Leviticus have attracted critical analysis for over 2,000 years, from the Hellenistic era when Greek thought based on the idea of natural reason was brought to bear upon them and theorized that the most delicious animals were the ones permitted, there were also the ethical theories, and the medical theories which remain popular to this day, with the anachronism of knowledge of trichinosis being projected back onto the undercooked pork of long ago. However, Douglas' analysis found an obsessive interest in classification, of ordering, and an especial orientation to excluding hybridity, animals that in some way challenged the culture's ordering principles. These principles came from the Biblical God's creation; therefore, hybridity would be a violation of that. Cud-chewing, cloven-hooved animals were part of the Israelite God's covenant with his chosen people, and their nature and habits reflected that original ordering and covenant. The pig, cloven-hooved, yet non cud-chewing, violated this along with the camel; so did the hare which, with its constant chewing, appeared to have cud but was not cloven-hooved. The impure also incorporated creatures that violated their assigned category, such as sea creatures like eels that didn't apparently have the required fins, or any creature that swarmed or teemed, like most insects, and worms which were associated with death, corpses, the epitome of the defiled.

Julia Kristeva took this analysis further in theorizing the Biblical focus on defilement as evidence of a "tremendous forcing" of maternal power into the symbolic order in Lacanian terms in her *Powers of Horror*.[24] She notes that, while Isaiah had already stressed purity and impurity, it was with the Second Temple, the returning of the Israelites from the Babylonian Captivity, that these oppositions became fundamental to Jewish religious life. In a way that would have seismic reverberations for future historical development, the Babylonian Captivity shaped the development of monotheism, as the religious life was molded by a great sense of the people having transgressed and so deserving such punishment.[25] She argues that material abomination and the topological (here the religious life of the Temple)[26] are two sides of a coin: "The one and the other are two aspects, semantic and logical, of the imposition of a strategy of identity, which is in all strictness, that of monotheism." The human is completely set off from the Deity, with the first dietary prescription being laid down in the expulsion from Eden.

Kristeva sees these all as essentially about separation, the separations established by the symbolic Law of the Father, and she goes further to link these to the development/establishment of subjectivity.[27] Death is viewed as especially defiling. "A decaying body, lifeless, completely turned into dejection, blurred between the inanimate and the inorganic, a transitional swarming, inseparable and lining of a human nature whose life is indistinguishable from the symbolic—the corpse represents fundamental pollution."[28] The corpse is waste, it is the mixing of categories and the challenging of the symbolic and God's law.

If the root of systems of the pure/impure lie in the horror of death, especially the immediately present corpse, rotting, perhaps teeming with maggots, and stinking, not the clean bones of the ancestors, but the disturbing confrontation of our mortality, in this sense death is disruptive. It's important to not project back into earlier times our modern knowledge of viruses, bacteria, and other microbiological agents of disease. In death's appearance our identity can be shaken, even if momentarily, and this involves the shuddering of our symbolic cultural-linguistic codes of meaning. I see a black plume of smoke rising from the crematorium on a warm fall day as I stand in the sun of the parking lot, and there is a momentary breakage—that is the smoke of my friend's burnt remains. However, it passes quickly as the smoke dissipates, a clean dealing with corpse. An ashy, purified residue left behind. Perhaps the widespread repugnance with death and the hemming of it with taboos of purity are rooted in the intense reminder it gives of the materiality of the body with its mortality, and the linked view of both birth and death being so twined. The dead must be turned to Ancestor, and the cast off decaying corpse hid with its unpleasant reminders of animality, of that which is solid liquefying in fecund rot,

---

24 Kristeva theorized a semiotic that is something like the pre-mirror state of the child, and associated with the mother, as opposed to the symbolic order of history, sociology, and assigned meanings, the Law of the Father. Yet unlike in Lacan's thought, it continues to break forth in poetry, in prosody and rhythm of language and music.

25 (Kristeva 93)

26 Kristeva maintains that with the Second Temple came the emphasis on abomination, the ferocity of symbolic order, and the abjection of the remainders, all that must be excluded; it passed from a sacrificial religion to a moral one. The sacred was delimited to the One, strictly the right-hand sacred: "at the limit, everything that remains, all remainders, are abominable." It was a radical shift.

27 (Kristeva 94)

28 (Kristeva, 109)

LEFT SACRED

of the dissolution of the basic dichotomy humans have made between them and the other myriad of life. "We have no greater aversion than the aversion we feel toward those unstable, fetid and lukewarm substances where life ferments ignobly. Those substances where the eggs, germs and maggots swarm not only make our hearts sink, but also turn our stomachs."[29] Life and Death terribly mixed, all mixed up. The most basic categories rupturing, confused, fermenting.

If the corpse is the ground of impurity, it may seem surprising that Birth is also the subject of such ideas of pollution, of the impure, of what the Greeks call miasma. But again, basic ordering principles are cast aside, undermined, ruptured in the event of birth, the mother's body violated by the emergence of an other, paralleling the violence of the worms and grubs who transmute the corpse flesh. "Like excrement, the mother poses a threat to the identity of the body, to its autonomous corporal limits..."[30] All associated with the violence of Death, the disruptor of the cultural world of work, of making tools. Since in archaic times, and in many present or near-present tribal cultures, all deaths were perpetrated:

> Death was a sign of violence brought into a world which it could destroy. Although motionless, the dead man had a part in the violence which had struck him down; anything which came too near him was threatened by the destruction which had brought him low. Death presented such a contrast between an unfamiliar region and the everyday world that the only mode of thought in tune with it was bound to conflict with the mode of thought governed by work.[31]

The supernatural force that has seized the dead person and has disordered the "course of things does not cease to be dangerous once the victim is dead." It lingers and can assault those living; in other words, it is *contagious.*

Since Durkheim,[32] there's been a recognition that not only do religions separate sacred and profane, but that the sacred itself is dualistic: there is a beneficial, positive, right-hand sacred, and a dangerous, chthonic, left-hand sacred, a pure and an impure sacred. Durkheim forged an understanding of the sacred as dual (though first posited by Robertson Smith): the pure right-hand sacred of heaven-oriented religions, of the institutions of the type familiar through Christianity; and the left-hand or impure sacred, characterized by the destructive, and the tabooed, perhaps most familiar through Tantrika practices. The term sacred originates in Latin sacer, which had both meanings, the "set aside" could be the conventionally holy or it could be the accursed (in languages derived from Latin, sacred still contains both meanings, the accursed being a form of the sacred). Students of Durkheim such as Marcel Mauss, most known for his work on gift economies, didn't necessarily see this duality as of separate realms, but could be two aspects of the sacred, the left sacred seen most clearly, perhaps, in sacrifice. The tremendous force of breaking tabooed behavior showed in such times as festival and the death of a king. According to the College de Sociologie, a 1930s group established in Paris to study the sacred founded by Georges Ba-

The removal of impurities is an elaborate quest of separations, a ceaseless maintenance of identity, a structuring of language and matter.

---

29 (Bataille, *The Accursed Share* 81)
30 (Direk 196)
31 (Bataille, *Erotism* 46)
32 Emile Durkheim elaborated on the left and right sacred in *Elementary Forms of Religious Life* (1912)

taille, Michel Leiris, and Roger Caillois, the sacred was seen "as radically opposed to the profane or everyday as well as acutely ambivalent, internally divided between pure and impure, beneficent and dangerous, right and left aspects."[33] It is dangerous to the normally stultifying orders we live within.

Someone has been seized by death: to stop its spread, Death must be propitiated—and that means dealing with infernal, impure powers, and those others that may require transgression of purity in the dark sacred, and thereby paradoxically a part of death. In Greece, the chthonic powers were approached by the defiled with mussed hair, with lamentation and blood poured into a pit, pretty much the opposite of the Olympians. Instead of white animals, black ones were sacrificed.[34] Release from normal rules of order and purity were found in Dionysian rites, of maenads slipping out of women's usual confined state into forest and mountain raving, and omophagia, eating the raw meat of sacrifice.[35] In the Celtic world of Gaul, shadowy deities are called to covens of sorceresses in the Larzac Tablet,[36] revealing left sacred practices. Irish lore is replete with dealings with the dwellers of the sidhe mounds, the dead, and visionary poetry is found on grave mounds, in darkness, and young poets arise out of fugue states like Amergen in the story "Does Greth Eat Curds."[37] The poet in the making is filthy, defiled and in communion with chthonic and marine powers. Around the world practices for breaking ordinary order abound, with the practitioner conscious of the social nature of an order that must seem

33 (Biles 4)
34 (Burkert 200)
35 (292)
36 (Koch 3-4)
37 (Thompson 138-9)

LEFT SACRED

simply reality to the ordinary person." So we can see that the left and right sacred are sides of the same coin, or on a spectrum. In Sumer, in the story of the descent of the goddess Inanna into the Underworld ruled by her dark sister Ereshkigal, who has her hung up like a carcass on a butcher's meat hook, she receives the aid of the non-binary beings called variously *kurgarra, galatur,* and *assinnu* who were said to have been created by the god Enki from dirt under his fingernails. They were lived in human roles by gender-variant male-bodied priest/esses.[38]

Besides Dionysos, perhaps in western tradition there's no more exemplary deity of the left-hand sacred than the late classical Hekate. While in earlier days the chthonic (and once celestial) goddess received household and shrine leavings and sweepings put out on the nearest crossroad, by the early centuries of the Common Era she specifically took those substances considered defiled in systems of dirt and cleanliness, for example being offered cow dung incense[39] and even a "perfume" made of goat fat, baboon shit, and garlic.[40] She is even seen as a devourer of corpses, that most polluted of objects; as Hekate Borborophobia, the Eater of Filth, she was addressed.[41]

The understanding of the left-hand impure transgressive sacred has largely been left out of the understanding of contemporary Paganism/polytheism to our detriment, and leads to the appearance in recent times of panics about miasmic contagion. The forms of the heterogeneous sacred are limitless but often are of bodily fluids, of rot, of excrement, of flows and eruptions of the body. They violently transgress the rational, the utilitarian, and puncture the flat world with which modernism/capitalism has pervaded the planet. The idol sedimented with blood and ghee is a traditional image; the headless Acéphale[42] of the Bataillean secret society is a modern one.

It is interesting to consider how rules of tabooed and impure behavior were suspended at certain times, such as after the death of a king. For example, reports from Hawaiian kingdoms show the whole system of order, of pure and impure, crashing after the death of the one who personified it.[43] The headless sacred emerges in the loss of the leader. It's worth considering that "capital" etymologically is derived from head (the Latin caput); the sacrifice of the headless sacred can lead us elsewhere. Contemplating such applications to our own world and developing praxis is timely; a confrontation with impure heterogeneous sacred matter can help take us somewhere better, bursting into alternate worlds.[44] The disordering, the rupture of firmly held identities,

> not only do religions separate sacred and profane, but that the sacred itself is dualistic: there is a beneficial, positive, right-hand sacred, and a dangerous, chthonic, left-hand sacred, a pure and an impure sacred.

38   (Conner 70-2)
39   (PGM: 4 1438-40)
40   (PGM 4: 2455-66) (qtd in Rabinowitz 62)
41   (Rabinowitz 62)
42   Acéphale is both the headless mythic person and the name of the secret ritual group founded by Bataille, which could be thought of as the inner mystery of the outward political College de Sociologie. One aspect of the headless is that of a non-authoritarian reclamation of myth, as opposed to the headcenteredness of fascism. See Allan Stoekl's "Introduction" to Bataille's *Visions of Excess.*
43   *The Accursed Share* (89)
44   I think the outer model of the College de Sociologie and the secret society of Acéphale offer models very relevant for our time.

the shuddering of the impure sacred, are the shifts we need in a world awash in industrial pollution, racist oppression, misogyny, compulsory heterosexuality, extinction, and hyper-capitalist exploitation. And it's more than time we shape our paganisms/polytheisms with the awareness of the power of the left-hand sacred.

I will end with a short tale.

The sirens were on, security had been breached, an automated voice demanded clearance of the structure. But one scientist didn't evacuate, ignored his colleagues' stern gestures as they departed; perhaps he'd been infected by the virus that was rumored to be sequestered in the institute's basement. A violation of protocols, but he stayed on seeing a beast manifest, a hippopotamus it seemed, no, it was shifting into a pangolin, or was it a sow giving birth? He reeled, glasses falling off, staggered. Now a woman turning into an eel, then a slime mold, kaleidoscopic and iridescent and it was Abraxas and then a dancing decapitated man and...you get the picture. The scientist had dropped his lab coat, in fact he stripped naked and was ruptured in a mystic experience, his self lacerated in an ecstasy. Afterward, they said he was filthy but his smile blissful. That world was never the same.

FINNCHUILL

Finnchuill is a Celtic polytheist, a poet (fili), a druid, an animist, a Dionysian. This queer polytheist-at-large blogs at finnchuillsmast. wordpress.com and writes for Air-N-Aithesc, (a Celtic pagan magazine), and is the author of a book of mystical poetry, From the Prow of Myth. Finnchuill works as a college educator and is currently living in the US-occupied nation of Hawai'i.

The Gods of My Ancestors

Anthony Rella

"I got an image of you," he said lying next to me. We were naked and enjoying the luminescence of limerence, those early days of high hormones, great sex, and mutual fascination. His hand passed over the length of me, not touching me, sensing my subtle body. "I think it's a past life. You're in ancient Egypt. You're wearing simple clothes, like you're a peasant."

I'd been Pagan for about two years and was still figuring out what that meant. After years of seeking connection with spirituality through Catholicism, I'd found in Reclaiming witchcraft a welcoming, queer-affirming, ecstatic community that offered me tools and practices that were waking me up in new and powerful ways. What I continued to long for was a connection to the divine, to the Gods.

"That's interesting," I mused. "We all did this meditation once to our Places of Power. Mine was all black, black skies and black sands, with a giant black pyramid in it. And I was in jackal form. It seemed very Egyptian."

Not only did it seem Egyptian, but when eventually I pushed myself to start doing actual research, I learned that the older name of Egypt, Kemet, translated as "the Black Lands." Every time I went back to that Place of Power, I saw images of Anubis: hearts growing on trees, jackals.

A few months after the bedtime vision with my lover, I took another trance and met Anubis, who said, "I'm waiting for you." I'd been waiting for a God to "claim" me, assuming that's how it worked, and still it took me a while to get what Anubis was trying to tell me: the Netjeru had been waiting for me all along, giving me gigantic flashing neon signs pointing in Their direction, but it would be my job to follow the signs.

Part of my confusion and unwillingness to answer the call came from not knowing "which" gods I was "supposed" to honor. Some liberal and conservative Pagans suggested I should start by "honoring the gods of your ancestors."

The Delta of Many Legacies

I am a white man. My known ancestry is German, Irish, and Italian with some Sicilian. My paternal Italian and Sicilian ancestors were the most recent to come to the United States during the early twentieth century. My grandparents were the first generation to be born in the United States. My grandfather enlisted to fight in World War II. Fortunately for him the war was coming to a close, so he was deployed to Germany to oversee the postwar peace process. There he became interested in German culture and tried to learn the language. He'd tell us about the women who laughed at him when he mispronounced "Ich heisse" (My name is) as "Ich scheisse" (I shit). Much later in life, after retirement, my grandparents traveled to Germany and Austria, and grandpa ended up president of his local German club.

Their son, my dad, grew up in New York and Connecticut, as most Italian-Americans do, but decided to go to college in Indiana. As an adult, now knowing Indiana and New York, I do not understand his choice, but I get the urge to branch out from your family for a time. There he met

> What I continued to long for was a connection to the divine, to the Gods.

and ended up with my mother, an Irish-German-American who grew up in Indiana.

On her side, we have records of the German family in the United States going back to the 1700s. At one point they were Pennsylvania Dutch, so for a long time I thought that meant we had Dutch ancestors too. Apparently it's a misnomer. They were actually *Deutsch* which is German for "German." United States whiteness mutated their language and names, as it does. The family ended up owning farmland in northern Indiana in a town with a road still named after them. My grandfather from that lineage grew up Lutheran but converted to Catholicism for my Irish grandmother, herself a Maloney, a surname translated as "descendent of a servant of the Church."

My mother's father, too, served in World War II, though his fortune was quite different. He was deployed to the Pacific to fight the Japanese and involved in Iwo Jima. Our grandmother told us a story about being at a party while the men were deployed, during which they broke plates because they had been made in Japan. My grandfather returned with several hallmarks of post-traumatic stress disorder and rarely spoke of his experience. Unlike my other grandfather's expansive relationship with culture, my mother's parents had an insular nativism and unquestioned prejudices against nonwhite people, freely using bigoted language even when it shocked my generation.

Catholicism gave my parents common ground, though Irish and Italian Catholicisms are quite different. Irish Catholicism brings a lot of the influences we negatively associate with Catholicism in terms of severity and denial of the body and sexuality, though it also evokes a high level of mysticism and awareness of the spiritual dimensions of reality. Italian Catholics seem far more about the culture, the pageantry, and the rituals that unite. In my experience, Italian Catholics listened to the guidance of their priests, bishops, and the Pope; then, they went to do whatever the hell they wanted; then, they came back for Confession and called it good.

The God of my recent ancestors has been Jehovah, the Christian God. My immediate ancestors prayed for the dead and honored a version of the divine feminine in Mary. Some of them believed that God, Mary, and Satan truly walk this earth at times, intervening directly in our lives. Some of them believe that Mary blesses her faithful, turning their rosaries gold to signify their devotion. Yet how could I honor a God whose churches said I was objectively disordered and living in sin as a gay man, whose teachings seemed increasingly out of alignment with my own truth? Yet if I did not honor that God, how could I feel at home with my family, who prays the rosary together in times of great need and crisis? These days, when Pagans and Polytheists say to "Worship the gods of your ancestors," most seem to include an unspoken parenthesis of "(except the Abrahamic one)."

Heritage, Seeking, and the Gods

I'd not had a particular interest in Egypt outside of my childhood, when I loved all the stories of the old gods. For one school project, I did a report in which I listed all the Norse gods I could find and what they were "god of," which I understand now is oversimplified and problematic but I was ten and not as wise at the time. The Greek myths, the Graeco-Roman overlaps, the stories of Christianity all intrigued me. As a baby witch trying to connect to ancestry, I looked to the Celtic, Norse, and Roman pantheons and myths to see if any of those Gods were interested in me. My community honored Brigid during Imbolc, and I felt a friendly affinity toward her. Another community that I worked with has a deep relationship with the Norse, but Freya and her kin seemed uninterested in me.

Roman religion was of a distant, intellectual curiosity, more for the questions it raised than the practices and deities associated. The Roman religion included practices of empire, in which distant gods were uprooted and brought to the capitol to ensure the empire's dominion over its outlying people. Gods whose lineages, teachings, and practices originated across the known world, reaching back even to Egypt, worshipping Isis, an Egyptian Netjeru who became exalted upon the world stage. Indeed, images of Isis nursing her infant Horus preceded or perhaps inspired later images of Mary with her infant Jesus.

The more I thought about it, the less it made sense to me to think I had any idea who the Gods of my ancestors were. Given shifting migratory, economic, and political histories, I couldn't say for sure that I don't have any ancestors that trace back to Egypt. Or maybe my soul reincarnated from a past life in which it was dedicated to the Netjeru.

At this point I'm less concerned about the explanatory models. I simply know these are the Gods who call to my soul, to whom I am called, and studying what I can of Kemetic history and practice inspires and nourishes me. What concerns me more is the need to argue with these explanatory models and teachings that ended up having little to do with my experience.

The other unspoken parenthesis comes into play when white Pagans talk about people of color working with their ancestral practices. Some white pagans think that if you have any Black, Native, Asian, or Pacific Islander heritage then "the gods of your ancestors" absolutely cannot be the European ones. As though the descendants of slaves, who were forcibly brought to this continent and experienced years of servitude and sexual violence by white masters that produced children, have no genetic lineage to Europe! This has nothing to do with spirituality and everything to do with a false attachment to ethnic "purity," a whiteness so fragile that any known drop of other ancestry pulls

> The same Zodiac whose symbols have been found inscribed in Kemetic sarcophagi, symbols whose roots go back to Babylon.

it out of the realm of whiteness. My father's sister has two kids with a Black man. Though we share the same Italian-Sicilian grandparents, would a white Pagan counsel them to study Italian witchcraft?

My Italian and my Irish ancestors were only granted access to whiteness relatively recently. Italians were subject to racism and lynching even into the earliest twentieth century.[45] The Irish experienced racial discrimination and oppression for years in the United States, until they were able to leverage white supremacy and political influence at the expense of people of color.[46]

I recognize, and get reminded when I forget, that I must humble myself in study and contemplation of a world and society for which I have little understanding. The Two Lands thrived for millennia, its remains still standing strong, but the teachings and ways of its people are very little like the life I have in the Pacific Northwest today. The Netjeru were as much entities of place as they are connected to the larger principles of life, the cosmos, and humanity. The inundation of the Nile is distant, I cannot comprehend its significance in a deep and direct way.

Transforming the Legacy of Whiteness

Not long after I began my courtship with Anubis, my father and his wife went to Italy so he could immerse himself in the language and research our family heritage. My sister and I were able to visit him

45   See Guzman's "The New Orleans Eleven: The Untold History of the Lynching of Italians in America," and note that this does not mean Italians went through racial discrimination equivalent to Black or Native people: http://www.globalresearch.ca/the-new-orleans-eleven-the-untold-history-of-the-lynching-of-italians-in-america/5372379

46   Please read *How the Irish Became White* by Noel Ignatiev

in Florence. I marveled at walking the same streets as Dante Aligheri. Perhaps I even walked the same streets as my ancestors, though the ones we knew of came from small towns. At the Baptistery of San Giovanni, my sister was surprised when I pointed out the Zodiac imagery painted in its interior. The same Zodiac whose symbols have been found inscribed in Kemetic sarcophagi, symbols whose roots go back to Babylon. Inside the neighboring Duomo, we lit candles and knelt in prayer. I knelt awkwardly, the old prayers feeling a poor fit in my mouth, but I knew I was in the house of the God of my ancestors.

"Dear God, I'm not happy with you," I prayed. "Your priests don't think much of me. But if you care for my family, then I will honor you for that."

After a few minutes I felt myself soften and begin to offer gratitude and respect for what I could. As much as I can bad-talk the Christian God and that religion's impact on my life, I'd never felt like I was at war with Him so much as with His followers. I sensed a beam of spiritual energy touching my heart, emanating from the altar. It was not a conversion or a moment of divine ecstasy; it was a rapprochement. I felt we were at peace with each other.

Looking at the depictions of saints and holy beings around me, noticing their own halos, I wondered if my Work wasn't so different from that of my Catholic ancestors and relatives. In my core witchcraft practice, we have a notion of what we call Self-possession, when the God Soul descends to permanently and immanently connect with the body and other parts of soul. Descriptions of this are of a sphere surrounding and intersecting the top and back of the head.

Here I am, though, being problematic again. As a white inheritor of Western culture, I've also gotten its legacy of attempting to erase difference and find some universal, transcendent culture that I can adhere to. This makes me more likely to look at foreign contexts and project my biases onto them, rather than humble myself to their difference.

And cultural purity is a bizarre concept. It defies millennia of documented exchanges and migrations. It defies how culture works, how it gets transmitted and transformed and reformed. How it becomes imprinted on the body, created through the body, transforms the body, but is not the body. A person who identifies as white in the United States has no claim to cultural purity. Whiteness is not an ethnic heritage. Whiteness is not a country of origin from which our ancestral practices, language, religion, clothing, and art emerged. Whiteness is a culture, insofar as it prescribes us to speak, act, believe, and dress in particular ways. It punishes those of us who do not conform, all the while trying to pass itself off as an apolitical universal norm. Cultural purity in the hands of whiteness is another weapon against people of color.

Whiteness is a culture, however, that has devoured its host mothers and become a parasitic monster that consumes other cultures, erases their origins, and then produces inferior products that it claims are its own invention. Yet whiteness insists upon its own superiority, the innate rightness of its economic and military supremacy. To honor the boundaries of other cultures, to humble ourselves to their difference and desires to differentiate themselves, is a resistance to whiteness and healing from white supremacy. It is a difficult labor of decolonization, one I struggle with often.

I have racist, sexist, and homophobic ancestors. I do them no disrespect by naming this. It simply is. They are also ancestors who served others, sought Truth, and reached beyond the limits of their cultures

> Cultural purity in the hands of whiteness is another weapon against people of color.

to build friendships. They are ancestors who ventured beyond the bounds of the known to enter new lands. I have ancestors who were human beings, who danced and sang and made love and hurt each other. What I don't have are racially or culturally "pure" ancestors. So I honor the Gods of my ancestors of blood and spirit, all of them, all who care about humanity and our place in the cosmos.

ANTHONY RELLA

Anthony Rella is a witch, writer, and psychotherapist living in Seattle, Washington. Anthony is a student and mentor of Morningstar Mystery School, and has studied and practiced witchcraft since starting in the Reclaiming tradition in 2005.

HUNTER HALL

Hunter Hall's a ferocious poet seen late last century lurking black-hooded about the rainy streets of Seattle. Reading Deleuze & Guattari while slinging brutal mochas, channeling serpents and raw riot through her spoken-word performances, she now lurks somewhere in the Salish Sea, plotting revolution while baking for her children.

Yellow Tape & White Carpet

Hunter Hall

I grew up haunted
unwanted
except by
the bog lady
leading me to her special
spot for the best cranberries.

Come, little girl…
I have a secret to tell you.

(crawling under the beams
cheek pressed tight to the dirt
clawing cobwebs from
my eyes
I realize that
I am my own bar with
KEEP OUT
DON'T EVER GO THAT FAR
written on it.)

I grew up possessed
distressed
swallowed by memories
dipped in head first.
My mind is a cup
that is overflowing
sploshing all over
the fancy white carpet.

(And Lo! An angel
appeared
and whispered
*secrets that I have **forgotten**)*

I sleep
and dream
of unrelenting glimpses
of happiness.

(memories slip up
like gas trapped in a tar pit
telling me all those secrets
again and again.
always too late to prevent
the slackjawed
train wreck I create)

I grew up haunted.
Unwanted.
I dream that that will change
that I will be seen.
Heard.
I grew up, but not out,
trapped in that
bog or tar pit
only glimpsed
in nightmares
and torn fragments
of hazy memories.

(look at me,
come on,
see me.)

It will never be me,
for I spilled my
heart's blood all over
your fancy white carpet.
and I have no more
to give.

LEFT SACRED

Fear & Loathing
at the Crossroads
Dr. Bones

The events of that strange and terrible evening are doomed to stick forever to my soul, and even as I hurriedly type these words I can feel my glands twinge with dread. In the service of Gods & Radicals I had called upon the Otherside for wisdom, but was left struggling to put into words an event that seemed to defy all of them. All I knew for sure was that I'd ventured to some imperceptible edge, been taken to the heights of hosanna and snatched away before I could lay my hands upon the golden goose.

These are the events as they happened to me.

It was September the 11th in the year of someone else's Lord, and I was at a shooting range sending small metallic beams of death towards a target 15 feet away. On a day of solemnity I was determined to make as loud a racket as possible, each bullet in my mind not ripping through paper but federally paid-for body armor.

I had of course been drinking heavily.

"The idea is pretty simple!" I shouted at my wife in between rounds. "I'm going to get under the influence, start tripping balls, and then head on down to the crossroads to speak with The Man there about what he thinks about us!"

Who was this man? *Who* he is exactly is hard to say. He's a Hoodoo original, a distinctly American god, a cousin to Eshu and Legba borne across the middle passage and brought up in the South East. Under palm and pine he has been whispered to for time immemorial, lurking in every town with a lonesome crossroads or weirdly vibrating intersection. He is a teacher, a guide, a syncretization of the pact-making European Teufel and the crossroads deity of Mother Africa. He is Yog-sothoth and Nyarlathotep with a southern drawl and 1930s flair.

To the uninitiated he was the Devil, Satan himself risen out of the ground and looking to lead the faithful astray. Ole Nick' haunted lonesome roads across the South, appearing as strange animals and teaching secrets to witches hell-bent on ruining the lives of good, day-time folks. Oils with names like "Black Pact" could be used to grab his attention, and old-school practitioners were said to bury cats alive in his honor. For a Southerner of the old days to witness someone out at the crossroads on a moonlight night was to come face-to-face with nothing short of an enemy of Yahweh, a warlock opposed to all "natural" things like law, order, and anti-miscegenation laws.

All of this might have been true, and probably was, but it was only half the story. One of most dreaded aspects of the Crossroads Man was his quintessential African nature. The author Erik Davis in "Trickster at the Crossroads" would note crossroads gods shared "many obvious trickster elements—deceit, humor, lawlessness, sexuality."[47] These intelligences however weren't merely pranksters but gods of "communication and spiritual language" sharing the eldritch title of "gatekeeper between the realms of man and gods, the tangled lines of force that make up the cosmic interface." The Crossroads Man held "the power of ambiguity and the multiplicity of perspectives" that could "change the fixed into the free," and as such had been the impetus to many a Conjurer's career.

That power was sorely needed today more than ever, and was the purpose behind my hedonism. Your average American was in such a deplorable state it was enough to make one vomit: union membership is at an all time low,[48] and 79.7% of all laborers work shit-pay service jobs.[49] To add insult to injury, the American worker hasn't seen her wage increase since 1979[50] while the prices on everything from food to housing has gone up. Victories against this death march are as hard to find as clean water in the Tampa Bay. The bones of Occupy and a host of other social causes, once buoyant, lie bleaching on the plains. The human species appeared straddled to a dying planet and every attempt at liberation, save for a few, had its brains firmly dashed against the rocks.

Perhaps maybe it was time for a new view, a new perspective, one wholly inhuman and removed from the petty power politics so peculiar to revolutionary struggle. Who better to ask about the downfall of capitalism, patriarchy, and the whole legion of spirits that kept humanity in bondage, than a god so rebellious he healed the sick, cursed the innocent, and broke every stagnant pattern His gaze happened to gather on?

But a wandering mind is not good for hands holding a loaded pistol, and I struggled to remain focused on the task at hand. I needed my attention on this cardboard fucker I'd set sights on, his gas mask and unnerving authoritarian disposition marking him as some two-dimensional member of law enforcement. Gently, ever so gently, I squeeze the trigger as a sonic boom rips out of the muzzle in an ecstatic release somewhat close to an orgasm.

My momentary distraction has caused me to miss my target's eyes, yet somehow I've hit him in the groin. I count it as a bulls-eye.

I pack up the target paper with the idea I might

For a Southerner of the old days to witness someone out at the crossroads on a moonlight night was to come face-to-face with nothing short of an enemy of Yahweh, a warlock opposed to all "natural" things like law, order, and anti-miscegenation laws.

47   http://www.levity.com/figment/trickster.html. Accessed 9/14/16

48   http://www.npr.org/sections/money/2015/02/23/385843576/50-years-of-shrinking-union-membership-in-one-map. Accessed 9/14/16

49   https://en.wikipedia.org/wiki/Economy_of_the_United_States#Employment_by_sector. Accessed 9/14/16

50   http://thefederalist.com/2014/07/23/rising-prices-and-stagnant-wages-are-real/. Accessed 9/14/16

LEFT SACRED

hang it in the window as some totemic anti-theft charm, and leaving the firing area for the comfort of the "lounge." Soft cushions and chairs surrounded by an assortment of pistols, assault weapons, and dead animals encircle us while a cheap American flag hangs from the wall with its "Made in China" sticker carefully blacked out.

"So your essay is going to be about you and me?" my wife asks.

"No, not exactly." I pull a toothpick out of my messenger bag, making sure to keep my hammer and sickle bandanna out of view. "I plan on asking him about us, as in we anti-capitalists, in all our myriad of flavors. The Devil is the lord of the world, right? Well is he for us? Against us? Or woefully indifferent?"

"What do you think he'll say?" It was a question I too had pondered.

"To be honest?" I thrust my Brazilian made firearm back in my bag. "I have no fucking idea."

This account of magical misadventure would be read by many, so I wanted to do it right: once home I'd burn wormwood incense before I left and bring a big heap of it with me to toss into the road. Four candles would burn like torches on each end of the crossroads, and in one particular section I'd make a makeshift altar out of a bottle of fireball whiskey, a Joker from a fresh deck of cards, and a fork to stick in the ground. After that I wasn't sure what would happen, though previous experience assured me said creature would answer the call.

On to the potion. Inside a cheap plastic chalice hidden in the back of the cupboard lay the watery contents of Argyreia nervos, better known as Hawaiian Baby Woodrose Seeds. They had been purchased online, ground up, and soaked for 24 hours in purified water, a far superior method than than simply chewing them. The chemicals in the husks not only taste like the lower intestines of a rotten raccoon, but give the feeling that an entire tribe of sentient razor blades are dancing in your stomach when ingested.

Once I arrived home the brew was strained through a coffee filter and poured into a beer mug.

And there it sat for a good 30 minutes.

"What are you waiting for?"

"I...don't know. I don't know if I'm nervous or what."

"The longer you stall the longer everything is going to take."

"I know. I just wonder what's going to happen out there. I've done this before here, in the safety of our home, but I've never just walked around tripping balls out in the world before."

"Well, just make sure you don't get arrested."

And with that it was down the hatch.

Two hours came and went, the customary time for the LSA to start kicking in, but as of yet I had no reaction. I felt a little cold, true, but it seemed that this batch was a dud. Three beers and small pulls on 100-proof whiskey got my mind just liquid enough to float above the mundane, drifting thoughts stabbing out like harpoons as I lamented my position.

"What the fuck am I supposed to do now?" I asked in between spells of chills upstairs under the covers. "I built up all this hype on my Facebook page[51] and there's going to be no trip! I can't go back on that!"

I'm pretty sure my wife said something reassuring, at least I think so, but I can't remember. Suddenly I was seeing Nietzsche riding a skateboard while bob-

> Suddenly I was seeing Nietzsche riding a skateboard while bobbing his head to some kind of angry metal song.

51   https://www.facebook.com/TheConjureHouse

bing his head to some kind of angry metal song.

Well then, I mused, as my thoughts turned into colors,: it appears we have liftoff.

"Uh...hey....boo."

"Hmm?"

"I uh....I'm...the thing" I was struggling to use words as a kaleidoscope of colors unfurled like a flower into math equations. "..it uh....it's going."

"Okay," she chuckled, "I guess that makes sense."

I can't speak for other forms of LSA, or really other strains of Woodrose seeds, but what I was experiencing was a combination of pure MDMA and the interior shapes and thoughts of a mushroom trip. Inside me visions whirled and twirled as every cell in my body seemed to sing in pleasure. The blankets felt like the smooth velvet and my eye movements alone seemed to bring me increasingly towards orgasm.

I could have stayed like that all night, and in my blissful state I might have, if it wasn't for the large shadow that crept across my room. Unsure if what I was seeing was real I noticed every single one of our cats were watching it too, standing straight as arrows and eyes wide like dinner plates.

I gestured to my wife for a second opinion, my jaw rotating wildly in an effort to communicate to but it was too late. The shadow engulfed me.

The Man at the Crossroads had made a house call. Time itself seemed to stand still. Before me there was only a black mass, humanoid in shape, with a large brimmed hat. His presence, the strange kinetic

LEFT SACRED

energy that rolled off his "body," was as overwhelming as a storm making landfall on the Gulf of Mexico. The voice: soft but intelligent, bewitching and loaded mystery. Every word seemed to drop double meanings and open itself to a host of dizzying interpretations.

"I don't need or want your complicated ceremony. Come to the crossroads with that bottle of whiskey and you will have the answer you seek." My mind is still struck by the simplicity he sought. Unlike other deities, he desired no large table of offerings, no dead chickens, and I kick myself for discounting years of experience in originally favoring some flashy ritual.

A windup catapults the bottle into the air, the booze streaming into a perfect arc and appearing like an unlit molotov as it crashed into the ground.

Knowledge, the likes of which had puzzled theorists like Lenin, all at the cost of some cheap cinnamon whiskey. Who could ask for more?

Before I could speak he was gone as swiftly as he came. Bewildered, but enlivened, I sprung into action. Pants on, shoes on, another pull from the bottle of whiskey. I stop to think in my nine years of doing Hoodoo I've never attempted anything like this and I can feel my aura pinch with excitement. Fuck yeah, interdimensional reporting. A huge smile rips across my face, an eerily unnatural one, the kind that grows like pumpkin vines on a fool playing with dynamite.

Fear splashes across my wife's face. I am not myself. What was this madness?

No time to think. Out there at some lonesome intersection I can feel someone waiting for me. Tenebrous tentacles seemed to pull at my immortal soul with dread, but I had come too far to change course now.

Streetside, bottle of whiskey in my bag and four candles to mark the future ritual space, I struggle to appear as normal as possible. The roads are unusually crowded for 11:45 on a Sunday night, and I begin to worry I might have spectators ruin my ritual.

I did what any reasonable person would and began to shout at traffic.

"Go home you idiots! Don't you know this is a national day of mourning? Have you no decency?" As I feel my words rip through the air everything feels alive, like I've unlocked some hidden door. I grab my phone and record a poignant note:

"I am alive!"

Fifteen minutes of acting like a lunatic, but finally I reach my destination, and as I arrive the change in ambient atmosphere is nothing short of remarkable. No cars now, not even Pig Frogs croaking, the only witness a half-drunk moon lazily hanging over me. Spanish moss blew gently in the wind as the entire world seemed to hush itself to eavesdrop on my ceremony.

This gateway between worlds would have looked ordinary in the daylight, just an intersection with traffic lights, half-mowed grass, and plenty of empty bottles of Bud Light tossed by inebriated drivers. At night, as in all aspects of life, things change. Truths that can only be spoken in symbol are much louder when free from strict definition, and we are free to be anything we desire. Just enough light from streetlights to work by, just enough shadow to allow Things to slip in.

Of course every intersection would do the trick, and there was a long history in Hoodoo in using what you could. Here, however, there was some otherness, some perceptible delineation from normal reality that warned what looked solid was nothing more than a balloon waiting to be popped. You could feel it out here, The Weird, that feeling that caressed your skin and pulled at your hair and told you something strange was happening. Somewhere, either within me or without me, I heard an audible hum.

Gingerly I lit each glass-encased candle, placing it in a clockwise motion on each corner of the crossroads. Each one seemed to unlock a door as it hit the ground and the air around me began to feel looser. With the final one in place I stepped back, practically shaking from an electrical current I had somehow been plugged into. My eyes quickly began to quiver, my knees quaked, and as I prepared to call across the void I couldn't help but think the whole thing looked like something that belonged in an old school horror film right when the monster was about to appear.

Which is exactly what I wanted to happen.

I cleared my throat, took out the bottle of whiskey, and shouted the words that would rend the wall between worlds:

"Crossroads man, you who hold the keys to luck, money, love, and death! Hear my call!" I uncapped the bottle and held it aloft, feeling as if it had become a shining dynamo of energy. "I ask to speak with you, to speak with you about the people, your children, who are being exploited! What do you think about the people that are fighting against that!?!"

A windup catapults the bottle into the air, the booze streaming into a perfect arc and appearing like an unlit molotov as it crashed into the ground. To this day I still swear I saw sparks shoot out as it shattered into

> "What do you say to those that want to know if you are on the side of the Revolutionaries?"

a million pieces.

What then followed is a bit difficult to describe.

To any outsider, or potentially any good citizen that happened to be driving by, a thin man with a straw hat was gazing at empty space in an unnerving manner, jaw slack and eyes rolled in the back of his head.

As for me, I was in my body yet out of it, taken to a place that had no real name. Before me was Him in all his glory, at a distance yet taking up my entire vision. His presence was supremely alien, wholly unnatural and endlessly shifting. Coal black with signature hat, he spoke immediately in a tone that seemed to make every particle of reality shiver.

"I'm glad that my children are dancing, because ultimately that's what it is. If it were a different system they'd dance against it, too." In a flash of light I saw every critic, every muckraker, every indignant insurgent spread out across timelines connected as one. No solution was ever good enough, and it was their tireless hunger for more that continually pushed the world towards greater and greater heights. We fought, we danced, because to do so was to be alive. Renzo Novatore's words seemed to rise up like skeletons from a swamp and murmur in my ear:

> Every society you build will have its fringes, and on the fringes of every society, heroic and restless vagabonds will wander, with their wild and virgin thoughts, only able to live by preparing ever new and terrible outbreaks of rebellion!

The vision whispered implications: what if the struggle itself was the goal, the journey worth much more than the destination? How would your life, your dreams change?

Whether in the shape we know or some Euro-style "liberal" democracy, a primitivist village or a techno-fascist wonderland, the forces of Order and its allies will always seek to chain and enslave the human spirit. Each stone statue may be cut differently but is always incorrigibly rigid: hierarchy will always seek to reduce us to mere tools and society will always attempt to reduce us to the basest common denominator. Even if we get rid of these same powers, each new order will devise forms and methods to snatch the vitality of life from the throats of the living; as quickly as it was seized, power never really did go to the Soviets, and the grand general assembly refuses to hear my arguments unless I make the proper hand signs.

Uneasy now and unclear on the significance of what He was saying, I strained to form another question. The vision continued un-interrupted with Black Blocs and protests, rioting and demonstrations, variegated across time and space. I saw much and understood little, and my own stupor pressed me to speak again.

"What do you say to those that want to know if you are on the side of the Revolutionaries?"

His answer twisted in the air.

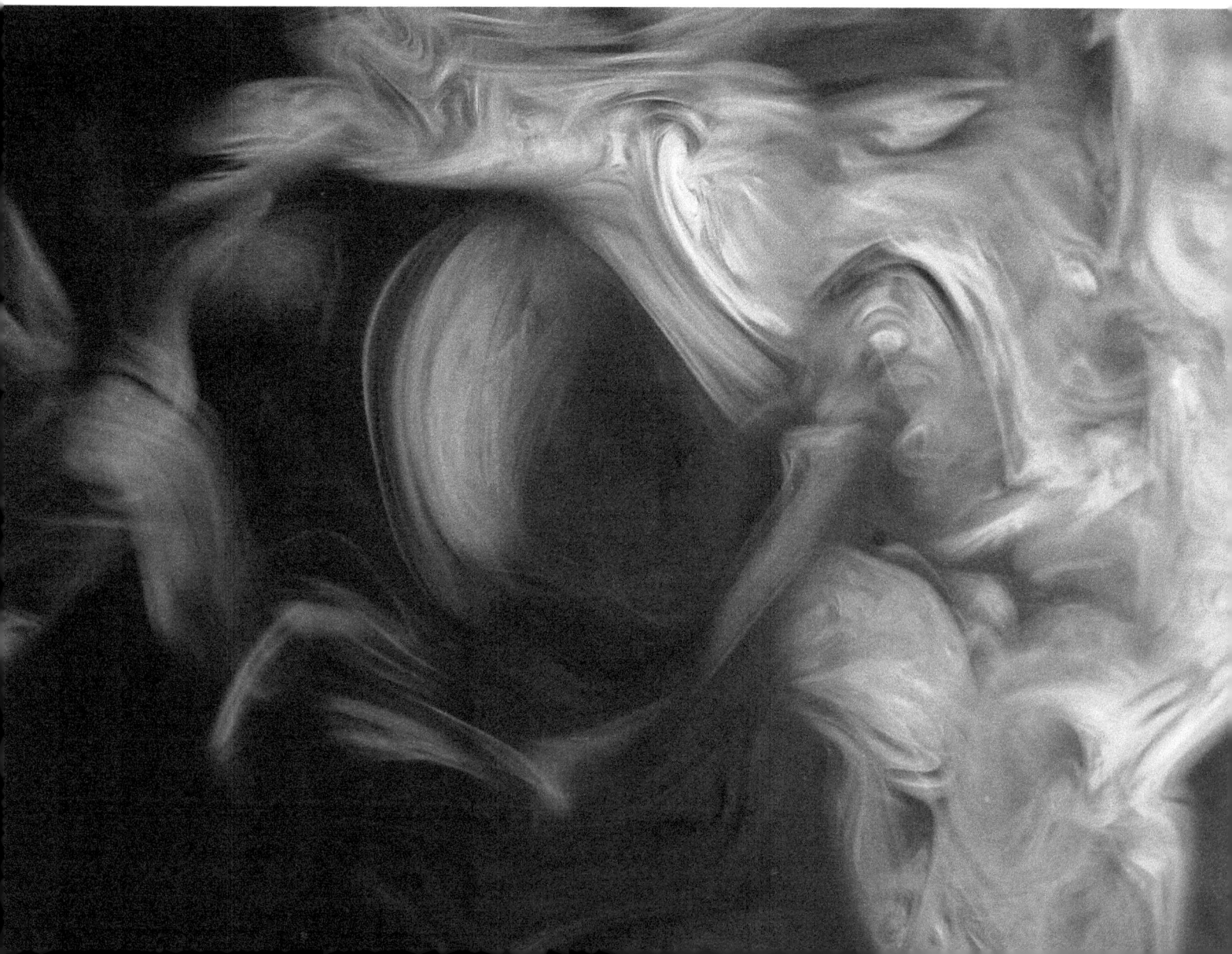

"I want them to know that there is nothing else than I would rather do/be[52] than fight alongside those people. There is something deep within them that I have implanted and there is nothing they can do to get it out. Those people are rebels, they are destroyers, they are creators. I nurture them."

"But why, why do you nurture them?"

"To build, to renew, to keep alive." Suddenly everything shifted. My eyes were seeing within me and I was staring at three graves freshly dug. From each a flower suddenly sprung. I was conflicted. Was all this all a game to him? What logic, even for a God, lay in endless conflict?

"So you cause turmoil in the world to keep it moving?"

He seemed to shrug his shoulders and gave a sense that my understanding was limited by my existence. Corpses and endless war were an unfortunate side effect of scheme upon scheme, and he made it clear both the planting and the reaping were under his domain. There was no joy in him at the prospect of murdered children, though he relished the opportunity to open paths afterwards for wrongs to be righted. I stuttered as the image of the graves melted away, trying to again ask just how we anti-capitalists of the magical bent fit into all this. He answered with thunder, growing displeased at my inability to understand.

"The sorcerers are the great changers, the great overthrowers. The destroyers of a world, they are children of an overturner. They want to remove, obliterate, and till new ground."

On my recording I can be heard uttering "Our struggle fits into his framework."

I can't accurately describe what this all meant, much less how it felt. Words fail to convey the…timelessness, the eternal nature of our struggle against a world pitted against us. I was shown that we fight a war as old as time itself, that we battle not against political ideologies but against calcification and rigid structure, a world of sharp angles and defined lines arbitrarily imposed to benefit a few. Society was by nature a sickly thing, top heavy and ruthlessly conditioned to weed out free thinkers who might oppose it. With a goldfish's intelligence, it stupidly sought to crush any semblance of the human spirit, the flowering of which was the only thing of value it could ever produce.

There was no mistaking it now. We were the disease sent to devour, the antibodies released to kill and maul a tumor. We were the lit sage bundle cast into

Where the Abrahamic gods decreed their followers accept reality as it stood and dare not question its wisdom, we wizardly folk were fated to critique, analyze, and dream; as the world jumped from leader to leader and system to system we would always be on the edge, a barbarous army of Occultniks wreaking havoc.

52   He said those both at the same time.

LEFT SACRED

the darkness to rebuke all that would wipe out all that was worthwhile.

I was shown, in a beautiful tapestry nothing will ever be able to capture, that the Devil himself and Lord of the Crossroads blessed our struggle, our fight. That that "thing" he "implanted" within us was a fierce hunger for a better life, a never ending fire that no water, free college, or wage increases could quench. Where the Abrahamic gods decreed their followers accept reality as it stood and dare not question its wisdom, we wizardly folk were fated to critique, analyze, and dream; as the world jumped from leader to leader and system to system we would always be on the edge, a barbarous army of Occultniks wreaking havoc. We rejected all consensual reality and substituted our own. Total victory was impossible because there would always be another battle, yet we would press on, sometimes failing, sometimes successful, but always ever forward.

I could have lived there, would have willingly let my soul be carried off to forever sit and hear secrets spoken clearly that humanity had only ever heard whispered.

But there would be no time for exaltation.

A cop car slowly pulled right in front of me to get a better look at just who the hell was roaming the streets this time of night.

I sensed it immediately, though I knew not how. Like a big fucking ugly freight-train shark rolling through water, its aura reeked of pure bullshit and aggressiveness. I snapped out of my trance and almost screamed due to my vision being cut short. I had left a land of infinite possibility and rebellious freedom only to be delivered into the hands of the Demiurge. So many more questions left to be asked, so many answers lost like songs sung at sunset. The cop car,

What if I told you the world gave birth to revolutionaries just as naturally as flowers, frogs, and trees?

appearing as both a gigantic living bullet and massive floppy dick drove through the crossroads, melting the massive array of energy and closing whatever gate I had managed to open. The human strip of bacon seemed to pause for a moment to look me over, and I was sure I would be spending the night in jail.

But he took notice of the candles, seemed to grow uneasy. Who knows what other weirdness he might have seen or felt? What legends might have echoed in his brain? Had the servants of the Devil once again taken up nocturnal roads best left untraveled? I'll never know, for as he drove off in a fit of fear I collapsed onto the street, struggling to put together the pieces of what I had just seen and gasping for breath.

What was supposed to be a fun interview has left me shaken, and days afterwards I can't say I've fully recovered. The effects of the LSA are long gone, but now I drink heavily. I have been to the edge and back and brought fire from the Witchmaster himself.

What if I told you there will be no utopia? What if I told you there will be no final victory, no joyous age of peace on Earth? What if I told you the act of struggle, that never ending battle for better and higher goals would never be achieved, but that every ounce of sweat we put into it would inch the globe ever closer to our impossible ideal? What if I told you we would never be happy, and that this was okay because the world would always need someone to call it on its bullshit?

What if I told you we were Diogenes, not Lenin, that our words would inspire no grand revolt but would march heart by heart forever through time? What if I told you the world gave birth to revolutionaries just as naturally as flowers, frogs, and trees?

The forces of death and stratification will always stalk the streets, gun in hand, just as surely as that cop car drove by and put an end to a beautiful, incomprehensible freedom. But in an endless cycle of conflict, there is hope. Just as plainly as these constricting pythons are fated to stalk the world, so too are we, and for every domesticated chihuahua that's born, a powerful she-wolf hellbent on living by her own wyrd-knowing is, too.

There will always be spaces and fountains where these wild creatures find solace, always be hidden corners where black magic roams and practitioners plot the downfall of the Daytime Kingdom of God. One remembers even in the depths of Nazi Germany there were roads, and, whether old or new, every pair that crossed paths held within it a new temple. He That Dwells Betwixt, the living avatar of change, eternally waits there gleefully laughing at the plans of all well-ordered men in uniforms.

And so I laughed, too, for it had always been and always would be; time itself became a flat circle and I walked home howling in joyousness at the impermanence of it all.

DR. BONES

Dr. Bones is a conjurer, card-reader and egoist-communist who believes "true individuality can only flourish when the means of existence are shared by all." A Florida native and Hoodoo practitioner, he summons pure vitriol, straight narrative, and sorcerous wisdom into a potent blend of poltergasmic politics and gonzo journalism. He lives with his loving wife, a herd of cats, and a house full of spirits. His writing can be found at Gods & Radicals, Disinfo, and Greed Media. He can be reached (and hired!) at DrBonesConjure@gmail.com and facebook.com/TheConjureHouse

ROCKET

Rocket is a gender-ambivalent, service-oriented transhumanist boi-thing, event planner, and anarcho-Jewish neo-hellenic witch who writes mostly poetry and prefers "it" pronouns. Rocket is part of a team creating structures of devotion to honor the queer and transgender Ancestors, which can be found at trans-rite.tumblr.com. You can find Rocket online at FlamingKorybante and in meatspace in Brooklyn, educating about and implementing non-carceral justice structures, licking boots, and definitely not starting a blood-orgy cult.

Prayer to the Mother(s)

Rocket

Hail, Ancestors.

Hail, fem(me)s, giants in your heels, offering us your shoulders.

Hail, queens, embodiments of every goddess throughout the ages,

Mothers like willow trees, Grandmothers with jewels between their lips,

and hail to the Maidens, uncountable crowds of them, fingers interlaced

and beautiful as a flame—hail to your pain and your parched throats,

and hail to the way you laughed.

Hail to the bois and the boys and the butches and the brothers and the

strength we may find in holding and bearing up.

Loves, the world is dry and desirous of tearing us apart.

It wants to drain us and then drag

until the muscles that hold our arms around you part like brittle leaves and

your lips on our foreheads become no more than a whisper. It wants

to crush our power and I swear to you—

for you, family, we will resist.

for you, mothers and sisters, we will smash the dams and let the water swallow the barriers between us.

for you, fathers and brothers, we will make our arms strong enough to hold tight.

for you, parents and siblings and beloveds, we will build something new--a world that would not have killed you.

A world that may not kill us. A world that will not kill our children. With one hand in yours

and one hand in theirs, shoulder to shoulder sideways through time

we stand with you. We honor you.

We honor your fear and your joy—

we honor the moments when you knew so truly that it bled

that this rusty world was not made for any of us.

Hail to the palms of your hands and the futures you imagined.

Hail to your fists and your teeth and your open eyes in the mirror.

Hail to the Mother of All who gathers her aching children into the circle of her arms

and offers them water, warmth, and rest.

THE SAFE HOUSE

Yvonne Aburrow

6pm, Tuesday

In the safe house, no-one uses their real name. It's safer that way. In case we get raided. There are several exits from the house, just in case. The windows are boarded up, so it looks like a derelict. There's also a hidden trapdoor. And we take it in turns to keep watch.

It's day 668 of the Trump presidency. Martial law has been declared. Hundreds of people have disappeared from our precinct. The gods alone know how many more in other areas, other cities. The TV only shows propaganda, so we don't know what's happening. We stopped using the internet when we realised it wasn't secure. The government took over all the internet service providers. Everything is samizdat literature now. We learnt a few things from history. How to copy out banned texts. How to lay our bodies on the line.

In the early days, the police let us demonstrate—while Obama was still in power, and before the purge. The signs of what was to come were in the Trump supporters grabbing women of color and threatening them—even before he had taken power.

A BEAUTIFUL RESISTANCE

I won't write my real name on this, but I go by Woody. This old guy who was here for a while said I reminded him of Woody Guthrie, the singer. I had a guitar but the police took it. They smashed it right in front of me, when I was singing at a demonstration. Back when demonstrations were still legal.

We are the Resistance. We carry out small acts of sabotage. Cutting wires, graffiti, the odd Molotov cocktail—when we can get petrol. People pass through the safe houses on their way to somewhere else—LGBT people, Muslims, women who have had an abortion or a miscarriage. I hope they find their way to safety. Canada, maybe, or Mexico.

It's been so long since I've seen daylight. I can't go out—too obviously queer as fuck, and I would probably get picked up by a patrol. So I sit here in the basement writing out samizdat literature by a fitful electric light. We tapped into a cable that supplies the local Trumpist office. They're not called the GOP or the Republicans any more—they renamed themselves Trumpists and banned all the other parties, including the Democrats.

There's a noise upstairs—better go and see what it is.

9pm, Tuesday

The noise was one of our newer residents, Taki. He brought in a trans woman. She was so thin you could see the bones sticking out. She escaped from a camp. She hasn't said much yet. Still shaking and crying. We had to feed her slowly, make sure she didn't eat so much that she would be ill. She's asleep now. I'll never forget the look in her eyes. Or the bruises.

I don't think she could really take it in that she was safe. Well, relatively safe.

It's like when some of the conscripts came back from building the Mexican wall. They looked like ghosts—dusty, exhausted, that terrible vacant look in their eyes.

1am, Wednesday

I prayed to Aradia, goddess of witches, goddess of the oppressed, to rise up and smite the oppressors. I hope she heard. I do know the ancestors are angry. I hear the dead whispering. When will it end? Why do the oppressors always win? When will the oppressed take back our power? Why didn't we do something while we still had time? Maybe somewhere there's a better enclave. Maybe it's true that California and Cascadia succeeded in breaking away. Or maybe their rebellion was crushed too.

All we have now is each other—the Resistance, the network of safe houses. I hope the rumors about the underground railroad are true. All we know is the contact for the next safe house. We don't know exactly where it is. Actually most of us don't know where any of the safe houses are exactly. When it's time to move on, you go to an agreed meeting point at midnight, and meet the contact for the other safe house there. Then they take you back, blindfolded for the last bit, and by a circuitous route so you couldn't find it again.

People pass through the safe houses on their way to somewhere else—LGBT people, Muslims, women who have had an abortion or a miscarriage. I hope they find their way to safety. Canada, maybe, or Mexico.

Because very few people can resist torture.

Must get some sleep. Difficult when you don't see daylight-- my sleep patterns are all broken up.

11am, Wednesday

Explosions in the distance—no idea what that can be. Could be fracking, but I heard they blew up a mosque in Chicago. An imam who stayed in the safe house for a while told me that. The Muslims have had a terrible time. People ripping off women's hijabs in the street. Rounding them up for deportation. Quite a few were raped. Those who tried to fight back were badly beaten.

The only hope is that the Trump regime will eat itself. It will run out of resources, overreach its supply lines, start too many wars, or maybe the rest of the world will finally do something. Though before the news blackout, it looked like the rest of the world was going to hell in a handcart. I hope those places got a better resistance organised. Some of them have more experience, I guess.

I have to finish copying the latest Gods & Radicals article. The runner is coming tomorrow to distribute it to the secret postal network. I'm not sure how that works, but I guess it is similar to how the safe houses keep in contact. Good thing that old guy stockpiled a load of carbon paper and typewriters and paper. I guess he knew the internet wouldn't last forever. People said he was crazy. He just laughed and kept right on saving them.

A lot of people knew a change was coming. Started making plans right back when Trump got the nomination. It's lucky really there are so many derelict houses—maybe they won't bother to look for us here.

Oh, here comes the runner now. I guess I'll stash this under the loose floorboard like I usually do. Oh gods, it's the police. Fuck.

Yvonne Aburrow

Yvonne Aburrow has been a Pagan since 1985 and a Wiccan since 1991. She has an MA in Contemporary Religions and Spiritualities from Bath Spa University, and lives and works in Oxford, UK. Her most recent book is "All Acts of Love and Pleasure: inclusive Wicca", and a forthcoming book on the inner work of witchcraft. She has also written four books on the mythology and folklore of trees, birds, and animals, and two anthologies of poetry. She is genderqueer, bisexual, and has been an anarchist socialist green leftie feminist for the last thirty years.

AGAINST THE WINDS OF HISTORY

Sean Donahue

The U.S. had just elected someone who will move us beyond the body- and soul-crushing policies of neoliberalism and several steps closer to unbridled fascism. The desperation of the people who, as James Baldwin said, "believe that they are white" to maintain the system of white supremacy is about to take on an even more brutal expression.

Whiteness was a concept invented to create a hierarchy between poor, displaced English and Scottish farmers sent to America to work off their debts, and the people kidnapped from Africa to work the same fields. Its purpose was to convince the newly-minted white folk that there was something in it for them if they kept Black folk down.

The descendants of those British peasants and millions more displaced from Europe by the violence and poverty that marked the rise of capitalism are now being told that their struggles for economic survival are the fault of new migrants from Mexico and Central America. They are being told there is something in it for them if they help carry out the rounding up and deportation of Brown people. They are being told they need more police and more guns to protect them from reaping a harvest of imagined vengeance for their complicity in the continuing genocides against Black and Indigenous people.

CNN refers to the water protectors at Standing Rock who are facing down tanks and guns with prayers as echoes of the "Wild West." Our President elect spoke in Nixonian code about "law and order" in response to Black uprisings in Charlotte and Milwaukee.

The carnage this country was built on remained invisible to those who profited from it for centuries.

Now we are living in a time where we watch it unfolding in videos posted on Facebook feeds. And, witnessing that brutality laid bare, the people who have believed that we are white, in overwhelming numbers, have said a clear yes to the ungloved iron hand.

Watching fascism sweep Europe in the spring of 1940, Walter Benjamin wrote:

> A Klee painting named *Angelus Novus* has an angel looking as though he is about to move away from something he is fixedly contemplating. His eyes are staring, his mouth is open, his wings are spread. This is how one pictures the angel of history. His face is turned toward the past. Where we perceive a chain of events, he sees one single catastrophe which keeps piling wreckage upon wreckage and hurls it in front of his feet. The angel would like to stay, awaken the dead, and make whole what has been smashed. But a storm is blowing from Paradise; it has got caught in his wings with such violence that the angel can no longer close them. The storm irresistibly propels him into the future to which his back is turned, while the pile of debris before him grows skyward. This storm is what we call progress.[53]

But what are wind and storm to witches?

But what are wind and storm to witches?

From within it, our culture feels propelled by irresistible winds of destruction. The linear narrative that history imposes on us, and the sense that all of time and space are contained within (and accounted for by) what we call history, feel like they will crush in on us. They feel like they will preclude possibility. We do not expect

53   Benjamin, Walter. *Theses Towards a Conception of History.* https://www.marxists.org/reference/archive/benjamin/1940/history.htm

LEFT SACRED

to weather the storm.

And it makes sense that our bodies respond that way. When we are overwhelmed and do not believe any escape is possible, we begin to contract and to surrender into death. If a black hole is a star collapsed inward on itself, creating gravity so intense that light cannot escape it, then trauma is its spiritual equivalent.

Walter Benjamin wrote of the angel of history as he saw the inescapable destruction of his own life approaching. But I have felt other winds and other storms.

Not even a sliver of all of time and space are contained in the stories we have been told about what has been, what is, and what is possible.

Most people throughout most of history have not lived under the grip of this terror. Capitalism and the ideology of whiteness are less than 400 years old.

People and communities, human and wild, were driven from the world by its onslaught. Those ancestors call to us, revealing in the music of their voices the rhythm and shape of worlds in which lives like theirs are again made possible. They rattle at the gates of death, demanding to be allowed to return.

Descendants, biological and cultural and otherwise, call to us as well, insisting that we shape a world in which their lives will become possible. They rattle at the gates of death, demanding entry into the world.

I have felt the winds that blow through when both gates are open.

But I have felt another wind too.

It is not theology, but fact, that every particle of your being and every particle of mine were present for the birth of the universe. When all things were contracted into a single point and exploded outward, the force left a curve in the structure of time and space that radio astronomers have mapped. The echo of that explosion is the background radiation they explore.

In my tradition, we dare to call that explosion orgasmic. We dare to understand our own being as infused with that ecstasy, and dare to explore our own role in the shaping of worlds. We are not powerless.

The force of that ecstasy blows stronger than the wind escaping the gates of the false paradise from which an upstart desert demigod exiled humanity. It rattles the bars and the walls of the prisons we have allowed to contain our imaginations.

The difference between trauma and ecstasy lies not in the source of their overwhelming power, but in whether we constrict against it or harness it and dance with it.

When we dance with ecstasy, we call worlds into being.

Despite the imminence of his own demise, Benjamin saw clearly the task at hand. He wrote:

> The tradition of the oppressed teaches us that the 'emergency situation' in which we live is the rule. We must arrive at a concept of history which corresponds to this. Then it will become clear that the task before us is the introduction of a real state of emergency; and our position in the struggle against Fascism will thereby improve. Not the least reason that the latter has a chance is that its opponents, in the name of progress, greet it as a historical norm. – The astonishment that the things we

> We dare to call that explosion orgasmic. We dare to understand our own being as infused with that ecstasy, and dare to explore our own role in the shaping of worlds. We are not powerless.

are experiencing in the 20th century are 'still' possible is by no means philosophical. It is not the beginning of knowledge, unless it would be the knowledge that the conception of history on which it rests is untenable.

At the same time that markets in New York and Tokyo and London are vacillating in response to electoral chaos—markets, which, we must remember, are driven by the monetization of the death of forests and deserts and human lives—the water protectors at Standing Rock are praying morning, noon, and night as they face down teargas and rubber bullets and armored cars in defense of the living world.

They know that their prayers are stronger than guns. They know that this is the work they were born for, the resurgence of a way of being the largest military and economic machinery in the history of the world could not drive out of existence, the return of understandings and relationships necessary to collective survival.

I am a witch, trained in a tradition that teaches that a witch bows to no one. I am wedded to gods far older than this planet, let alone this civilization. My body and my being partook in the creation of all things.

It comes down to this now: do we believe in the power of our prayers, our spells, our gods? And can we pray as fervently as the prayers arise at Standing Rock? Will we lend the force of our own beings to the same struggle?

Let us call in the storm that brings the real emergency.

And dance with its winds.

And dance with its winds.

SEAN DONAHUE

Sean Donahue is a highly neurodivergent wild forest creature who is currently an uninvited guest on the occupied territory of the Klickitat people in the Nch'i-Wàna ("Columbia") River Gorge. He is an initiated priest and carrier of the Green Wand in the BlackHeart line of the Feri tradition. He is also an herbalist. To learn more about his work go to http://www.seandonahueherbalist.com

SOLIDARITY NETWORKS
Gods&Radicals

Men brandishing assault rifles surround a building full of Black people. Groups of white men wearing biker's jackets bearing racist emblems roam the streets and make "visits" to Mosques looking for signs of religious extremism. A right-wing media figure shows up to a protest, his pockets full of ammo rounds, and aims a gun at unarmed women and children. Refugees from economic collapse and brutal wars flood across borders, risking drowning or getting smashed by trains and trucks to sneak through tunnels or over oceans.

None of these events take place in an imaginary future. This is our present world, one where all the illusions of peace, prosperity, and "civilization" are melting away. And this has always been the existence of the poor, of People of Color, First Nations, and occupied peoples in "the West" and the rest of the world—the rest of us are only now beginning to notice.

And it can get much worse. Probably will, especially after the results of a recent election. We're watching an empire crumble, and it's not going down without a fight. But before you despair, let me tell you what else has been happening.

Groups of people are smuggling fleeing refugees across borders—for free. Some show up when gangs of white supremacists gather in city centers and fight them off. Thousands of people are gathering on sacred land to help indigenous people fight off government-approved explosive pipelines. People are risking imprisonment and death to fight police, the military, corporate security, and fascists to defend others. They're stockpiling birth control, teaching self-defense, and working to keep other people safe.

There are many names for these sorts of groups. They transcend race and nationality, religion and family and community. They often also transcend class, and rarely fit squarely into usual political categories of left or right. And they seem to arise organically, always from the ground up.

They're called Solidarity Networks, and they are crucial to our survival. They're also crucial for building a new world from the ruins of Capitalism and Empire.

What's a Solidarity Network?

You're probably already familiar with Solidarity Networks, though you might not realize it. Actually, you already have the beginnings of one, but we'll get to that in a bit.

During the 1800s in the United States of America, abolitionists, former slaves, First Nations people, and sympathetic allies maintained safe houses and transportation for Blacks attempting to flee slavery into British/Canadian territory. This was the Underground Railroad. They did so without a specific hierarchy, and not only without help from the government, but in direct opposition to it. It was illegal to shelter fugitive slaves, even in so-called "free states." Another such network arose in Europe during the rise of the Nazi party and up to the end of World War II. Individuals and groups from many backgrounds and political persuasions sheltered, hid, and helped transport Jews out of Germany and Europe.

But helping fugitives is only one role of a solidarity network. In many cities in the United States, groups have been organized around helping immigrants and low-income folks (especially people of color) get wages from cheating employers or deposits back from deadbeat landlords. Similarly non-hierarchical, their members aren't just "activists": in fact, many involved are people who've been helped by former actions.[54]

What are the Traits of a Solidarity Network?

Regardless of the specific purposes of any Solidarity Network, they share the following traits:

They are intentional

While there are countless instances of people coming together to help others in need, a solidarity network isn't just a spontaneous action. Though they often arise organically, they are held together by shared principles and commitments and require organization.

They are distributed, rather than authoritarian

Solidarity networks have leaders and organizers, but the key to them is plurality. No one person is ever in charge of the network or the actions, but rather a group of people or, ideally, everyone involved. Not only does this prevent abuse, but it ensures that the network has more participation and can survive if something happens to core people.

They do not rely on government or the law

Solidarity networks are never part of the government. In fact, they often arise in opposition to the government, or to fill a need that the government cannot fill (or has caused). For instance, both the Underground Railroad and the many people helping to hide Jews during World War II were engaged in illegal activities. Others, such as SeaSol, use direct action to get justice where the laws have so many loopholes that official channels (such as the courts) always fail the poor.

They are political, but do not demand political conformity

The Underground Railroad was heavily supported by abolitionists, many who were early socialists. However, just as many were not socialists. You did not have to be a socialist or abolitionist to help, nor did you need to conform to any religious belief. Likewise, Socialists, Anarchists, Conservatives, and Liberals all worked together to get Jews out of Germany. While some political groups are much more likely to participate (and others likely to oppose the group), commitment to the cause is what is required, not identification with a party or political theory.

They make the most vulnerable their priority

Solidarity networks don't help the oppressed as part of their work, *that is their work*. This makes them radically different from many other groups (like charities, churches, or unions) who come together for other purposes but include justice. Solidarity networks start with injustice and center all their other activities around it.

What Are Solidarity Networks Not?

As mentioned above, a solidarity network is different from other groups. It's important to keep these distinctions in mind.

54   One strong and effective example is the Seattle Solidarity Network (SeaSol): http://seasol.net

They are not communities

Community is a word used so often it doesn't really mean anything. We use it to describe both neighborhoods and identity-groups—like Pagan or LGBT "communities"—as well as nebulous associations like the Online Gaming or Activist "Community." In all cases, community denotes a shared characteristic (living in the same neighborhood, playing online games) but not much else.

Solidarity networks are not based around identity, and do not rely on shared characteristics as a unifying principle.

They are not institutions

This distinction is pretty important. Charities, non-governmental organizations, non-profits, or other groups certainly do good work. Their downside is that they are top-heavy, slow, inefficient, and often rely on large groups of people donating money rather than time. Though a solidarity network might pool resources or ask for donations, direct action is more important.

They are not political parties

Though every single member of a solidarity network might be politically engaged and be active in political parties, the network is not a party. Political parties seek to gain power through the electoral process, rather than direct action. Electoral politics always leads to compromise of their founding goals and direct-action work.

They are not advocacy groups

A solidarity network doesn't try to "raise awareness" about the plight of the oppressed: it does something about it. While advocacy is often part of the work of a solidarity network, attempts to raise awareness are specifically used to bring more people within the network and to support their actions. Activism and advocacy are part of the actions, but not the actions themselves.

Principles of Solidarity Networks

No two networks are identical, nor should they be. But they do share several core principles, regardless of their differences.

Direct Action

Solidarity Networks do not rely on the electoral, legal, or political process to enact change. The people who hid Jews in their apartments in Berlin understood the political process wouldn't help them, just as the former slaves and abolitionists who hid and transported fugitive Blacks did not wait to win court battles or get the right people in office.

Direct action means action. It means doing something tangible to help others, rather than giving passive and indirect support. It isn't a Facebook like or a Twitter re-tweet; it isn't holding a sign or writing to your senator. None of those "actions" directly affect the situation of the oppressed. Likewise, Direct action is direct. It does not rely on the powerful, on representatives or officials or leaders.

We have become very accustomed to passive support: calling 911 when someone is in distress, giving money to large organizations like the Red Cross or Amnesty International. We cannot always directly help those in

A BEAUTIFUL RESISTANCE

76

need, but when we can, we must. And because we've become so passive, we will need to relearn what we are actually capable of.

Mutual Aid

Mutual aid is a principle very much forgotten in capitalist countries, and it's one we need to remember immediately.

Mutual aid is based on the idea that every person within a solidarity network is as valuable as every other, and each much be supported equally. This is seen best in the following two statements.

"An injury to one is an injury to all."

Every act of violence, oppression, and harm that affects an individual also affects the group. As in anarcho-syndicalism, solidarity networks make a commitment to support each person and to come together in their defense.

This is best seen in solidarity networks like SeaSol. Sometimes, those who became involved at the beginning to help others find themselves in the same situations as those they've helped. An activist might find themselves losing their job for unfair reasons and suddenly find people they helped helping them.

This principle is essential to the coherence of the group. Unlike communities formed around identity, everyone within a solidarity network commits to the well-being of everyone else. They are all allies, all accomplices, supporting each other whenever needed. Many oppressors isolate and target individuals: a group is always much stronger.

"From each according to their ability, to each according to their need."

Solidarity networks also recognize that each person has different abilities, wealth, privilege, vulnerabilities, and needs. Therefore, though they treat each person as important as every other person, they acknowledge some can give more while some will need more.

This is best seen in the networks who supported fugitive Jews and Blacks. Escaped slaves had no property, often could not read or write, and often had nothing to offer. Similarly, fleeing Jews had few resources, no access to more, and often didn't speak the language of their hosts outside Germany. In these cases, to expect the Jews or Blacks to carry their own weight or pay for rent or for food would have been more than unfair.

That doesn't mean they were unable to give back. Many escaped slaves returned to help others along the Underground Railroad routes, many Jews helped watch the children of their hosts or offered financial help in return. But since a solidarity network prioritizes the most vulnerable, it will acknowledge that those they help probably cannot help back during their greatest needs.

The Risks of Solidarity

Before we look at how we can build solidarity networks, we need to have an honest talk about risk.

We're not used to taking risks. In fact, if there's anything Liberal Democracy has been very good at is assuring us that it's always better to be safe, comfortable, and secure. Risk is for the foolish people, or for gamblers or stock market investors, not for everyday folk.

That's never been true for everyone. Life has never been safe, though if you're white, able-bodied, straight, or otherwise privileged, you probably aren't accustomed to the idea that helping someone might throw you in jail or lead to your death.

Get over it. Now.

LEFT SACRED

There's a massive chorus of Black, trans, queer, poor, disabled, First Nations, immigrant, and many other people who know that the safety and security promised by capitalism and democracy has always been a lie. It's never been safe for them—even if they toe the line, even if they obey all the laws, even if they pay their rent on time and never drive above the speed limit.

Right now, it's mostly just whites who still cling to this illusion. Worse, the refusal of whites to take risks on behalf of others is one of the reasons why oppression has continued for so long.

As Liberal Democracy collapses around us, whites are the only ones who really will have a choice to avoid risk. Stay silent, and you might be safe. Keep your head down, and you might not be targeted. Don't question oppression, and you might get to keep your jobs, your homes, and your normal life.

You might get to keep going as you did, while immigrants are rounded up and deported, more Blacks are murdered, vulnerable people die from lack of healthcare and medicine, trans people are beaten or kill themselves, First Nations people lose even more land and face down military-grade police forces... all for the chance that you might feel safe.

Do you really want that?

You don't, because you're still reading.

Ready? Good.

How To Build A Solidarity Network

Every solidarity network is going to be different, and it'd be useless for us to give you a prescription for what you should do. Besides, it's time to give up our hope that leaders know any better than us and can get us out of this mess. You are the leader you've been waiting for.

Though we can't give you a prescription, we can outline a framework. Tinker with it at will, play with it, use your imagination. This is broad enough that you can adapt it any way you need to, but specific enough that you'll hopefully understand what's needed.

1. Start with your friends

We wrote earlier that you already have the beginnings of a solidarity network. They're called friends, and they're awesome.

Think about your closest friends. If you needed something right now, they'd be there for you, right? And if they needed something, you'd be there for them. Also, you don't expect them to do the very same things that you do. They need different things, and can do different things.

Mutual aid and solidarity are not abstract principles. They're the foundation of friendship, and you're already really good at it. In fact, solidarity networks are radical friendships.

Also, you don't agree with everything your friends think, believe, or do. Maybe they vote differently, have different views on capitalism or religion or politics. But that doesn't stop your friendship, because friendship isn't based on those things. Neither are solidarity networks.

Think of a friend of yours who is as worried as you are about the way things are, hopefully someone who lives near you. Then, talk to them about what they need right now.

Ask them if they'd be willing to do something together to change stuff. Show them this essay if that helps. And then, together, talk about what you need from each other, what you can give to each other, and what you might be able to do together.

A BEAUTIFUL RESISTANCE

This may be an awkward conversation at first. Many people are not used to thinking of friendship this way. We take our friendships for granted, get lost in passivity of internet communication and the weight of the world's sorrows. But if you want to build something better, this will be your first step.

Don't worry, though. This is the easy part. They're your friends, after all.

2. Think about bodily and emotional needs

(DON'T SKIP THIS STEP!)

Another thing capitalism's been good at is distracting us from our bodies and emotions. We are often in our heads, thinking huge thoughts, worrying, fretting, plotting. So it's no surprise that so many people right now have been asking some very scary questions for the first time about how they'll survive all the chaos and violence as empire crumbles.

Ask the following questions of yourself first:

➤ What do you need to survive? Where does your food come from, your medicine, your shelter? How secure is all of that? What might happen if the way of getting that is disrupted?

➤ What do you need to feel safe? How many of the comforts in your life are only things that get you through the misery of your job? How much do you rely on police and the government for your bodily protection? What happens if that goes away?

➤ How do you deal with fear? Do you tend to shut down when crises happen, or do you put off emotions until the crisis is over? How do you manage panic, anxiety, depression, and despair? Do you rely on external sources (medications, entertainment, your friends and family) to get you through bad stuff, and what happens if they are not available in a crisis?

➤ What resources do you have? Do you have savings? A home, a car, other things that you might need if things get awful? Are you currently reliant on government income or benefits? What happens if those are taken away from you? Do you have any skills that don't pay the bills but could directly benefit someone in need?

➤ How do you care for yourself? Do you sometimes overextend your energy and resources? Are you good at communicating to people who support you when you need their help? Do you have trouble setting boundaries with people whom you support?

Once you've asked these questions of yourself, ask them of others. You don't necessarily need to directly ask them—you probably already know most of your friends' answers anyway. But to build a solidarity network, you need to understand not just your own abilities and needs, but those of others.

Thinking about your own situation and the precarious things that keep you safe will equip you to really understand the needs of others when they express them.

3. Extend out from your friends, and especially to people in need or danger

Solidarity networks are not communities. Communities are based on shared traits, while solidarity networks intentionally include oppressed people. Not only do they intentionally include them, they are built with them specifically in mind.

Here's the part where risk begins to come in. When you offer your support to someone in danger, you take on their danger. You share risk. Most friendships aren't based in unequal circumstances, but solidarity networks must be.

You don't need to go out looking for oppressed people. They are all around you.

You are probably quite vulnerable yourself. Be careful of the white liberal tendency to "adopt" tokenized oppressed people. That comes from living insulated lives, and only makes oppression worse.

Right now, you know someone who needs you. Maybe you know them only from work or the bar or your neighborhood. They might be the illegal immigrant who cleans your office or washes dishes at the restaurant where you work. They might be your Black neighbor, or the Muslim clerk at the convenience store where you buy your cigarettes. They might be the friend you haven't heard from in years, who you know suffers from deep depression, or your co-worker who just started transitioning gender.

Ask them what you can do to support them. Dare an awkward conversation, and risk the possibility that they might rebuff you or be facing problems so big you might be overwhelmed. Your network can't help anyone if it doesn't risk reaching out.

4. Use Your Privilege

You need to understand your privilege. That privilege might save someone's life.

If you're white, you should already know about your white privilege. If you don't, it's past time for you to learn. Most whites can walk by cops without getting shot, can walk into stores without getting followed. That's why many liberal whites don't take Black accounts of police oppression seriously—they don't experience it, and so have no reference point. Besides, they benefit from it.

To build solidarity networks, you need to give that benefit to someone else. You can't change the color of your skin, but you can acknowledge that your white skin can be used to protect the life of a person targeted because of theirs.

> If you're white, you can get away with stuff your immigrant or Black friend can't.

> If you're male, you're safer at night than your female friends.

> If you are healthy and have no medical problems, you can do things your disabled friends cannot.

> Straight and cisgendered? Your body can be used to protect your gay and trans friends.

This will also help you dismantle your privilege. Really listen to the needs of those around you, recognize their vulnerabilities, and use your lack of them to help them. Use your white skin to protect a Black person from a cop, your male body to protect a woman from sexual assault, your able body to gather resources and do work a disabled person cannot.

"From each according to their ability..." doesn't just refer to money or skill. Your privilege gives you access to things other people don't get. Use it to get it for them.

5. Grow, spread, seed

Keep going. The more of you there are, the more you can do. The more you succeed, the more other people will be inspired to do the same thing. And the more experienced you get at this, the more you'll be able to teach others.

There are some things to consider here, though.

Secrecy

If you're doing very risky illegal actions such as hiding immigrants or dissidents, you need what's called a "security culture." Every person involved in your network must commit to keeping your activities secret, must think beforehand what they will say if they are arrested, and must honestly consider how "an injury to one" will apply if they're being tortured in prison.

If your group gets large and relies on lots of people who are more "allies" than participants, consider the security culture of the Underground Railroad. People who ran safehouses rarely knew the location of many more of them, guides didn't always know each other, and slaves who were smuggled out didn't always even know the names of people who were helping them.

Such secrecy protected the entire network, and also helped get more people involved. If a fugitive slave was caught, no matter how much they were tortured, they could not reveal who was "behind" the Underground Railroad, because they didn't know. The same for any guide or host of a safe house. The entire network could survive because no one person knew all the secrets.

Beware of Authority

Your network is going to have organizers. More than likely, you'll be one of them if you started it. But there's a fine balance between being an organizer and being a central authority, and you must avoid the latter at all costs. This isn't just a matter of principle, though there are plenty of principled reasons to avoid top-down networks. It's a matter of survival for the entire group.

Police, military, mercenaries, and others will target the apparent leaders of a group. Being part of hierarchical, authoritarian groups themselves, they know how much chaos the loss of their own leaders would be. And if you have that kind of leader, the entire network can die when they are targeted.

As many people within the group as possible should share in the organizing role. That doesn't mean everyone needs to be an organizer, only that there needs to be several people able to fulfill the role at a moment's notice. Too much all on the shoulders of one organizer will crush that person anyway, leading to burnout, bitterness, and even the end of the network.

Prioritize Everyone's Needs—Including Yours

You can't save drowning people when you're drowning.

Every activist can tell you this, every organizer has a story. You'll be trying to help others, dedicating all your time and energy and resources, and then suddenly...you're done. You can't lift a finger, you can't be bothered to care. If it's bad enough, you actually start to resent or even hate the people you've been trying to help.

There are many reasons this happens, and it's a huge risk if you're one of the organizers of the network. If you have more "ability" to begin with, you may forget your needs, especially if you're trying to keep up a strong mood of hope against a world of despair. When others are looking to you for help, it's really easy to ignore your own needs, especially if others aren't in a place to meet them.

The point of a solidarity network is that everyone is supported. Make sure you are too, whether that's setting stronger boundaries with people whose needs are too overwhelming for you at the moment or taking time away from organizing, especially before you start to shut down.

What Now?

We've provided a very broad framework for solidarity networks, and used some specific examples to explain them. So you may be feeling a little overwhelmed. Are you capable of doing grand actions? Could you ever

LEFT SACRED

hope to be as courageous as others?

The examples provided were large for a reason. You are capable of all of that. You can save other people's lives, you can organize against bullies and the rich. And you may eventually have to.

But you don't have to start big. Here's a short list of places you might start.

➣ Medication networks: Many women, trans people, and medically-compromised folks may face a crisis over access to medications, birth control, and other necessary drugs. Do you have good health insurance? Don't need birth control but can get it? Access to pain, anxiety, or hormonal drugs that others might need? Build a network around this.

➣ Emotional care networks: Many, many minorities are terrified for their safety right now. Many are dealing with trauma and anxiety from what is happening and are feeling very isolated. Especially if you are worried but not yet directly affected by these crises, you can offer your emotional labor to them.

➣ Skill, tool, and resource share networks: These are very common already. You know how to do things that others don't, skills that may be life-saving to others. Most people don't know how to sew, to cook food from scratch, to garden—skills once basic to humanity but long forgotten by many. Self-defense is another one very essential, especially for women, trans people, and people of color. Even something as common as owning a car means you have access to something many people don't have and might need. Building transport networks for people in dangerous areas can save lives.

➣ Protection networks: Never underestimate the value of being physically present for someone in danger. Are you an intimidating-looking male? Imagine if you and four others all show up to stand in front of a Black or immigrant-owned shop that's being targeted by racists. You don't have to be armed (though it might be a good idea); physical presence alone can often stop attacks.

There are countless other ways of doing this, and your network might evolve as you continue. A group dedicated to teaching people how to cook might also be an emotional care network, or later commit to drive immigrant women home from their night-cleaning jobs.

Whatever you commit to, the most important thing to do is start now. And as you do, know that others are doing the exact same thing. Some of those networks will connect to others, some will be official, others clandestine.

And one final note. We mentioned at the beginning that solidarity networks are a key to building the world we want. This is how we can prove to others and to ourselves that we don't need authority, we don't need corporations, we don't need government and police.

Not only are we standing up to violence and oppression, we're building a new world, one that we know is possible, because we're from there.

Afterword

Lia Hunter

The English word "sinister" derives from the Latin word *sinistra,* which originally meant "left," but eventually became associated with "awkward" and "unlucky" as well as "evil." Conversely, the directional term "right" came to be synonymous with "correct" and "proper" and was associated with strength and authority. Since around 90% of humans are right-handed, leaving only 10% of people who are left-handed, we can imagine that left-handedness seemed like a disorder within the usual order, in an imperial society that seemed obsessed with order and regimentation.

In the Roman *avspecium* and Greek *ornithomancy* divination practices, one would read the omens of bird flight as good and lucky if the birds were flying in a rightward direction or to the right of the observer, and bad and unlucky if they were flying in a leftward direction or to the left of the observer.

The Early Ancient Greek word for left, *skaios,* and its Latin cognate, *scaevum,* appear to originate in a Proto-Indo-European root for "shadow" (*skaiwo). In many Indo-European languages, "right-hand side" also means "southward." Ancient Indo-Europeans and Semites both appear to have had a worldview that oriented eastward, where the sun rises as day begins. When one faces eastward in the northern hemisphere, the sun is always at some degree to the right-hand side and one's shadow then falls on the left-hand side. The northward lands—to the left, if east is your orientation—would be the lands where the darkness (*skot- in Proto-Indo-European) that is the root of the word "shadow" holds more of the day back, and gives longer nights.

> "In the best-known version of the Greek myth, Persephone is dragged down into the underworld by Hades, whose title is 'Pluto.' But in earlier, pre-patriarchal tales, she descends there under her own power, actively seeking to graduate from her virginal naïveté by exploring the intriguing land of shadows. 'Pluto' is derived from the Greek word *plutus,* meaning 'wealth.' Psychologist James Hillman says this refers to the psyche-building riches available in Pluto's domain. Hades, he says, is the 'giver of nourishment to the soul.'" - Rob Brezsny

You who have experienced the call and transformative ecstasy of magic and the exploration of the riches of the underworld and shadow are integrating them into wholeness in your being. You have begun to learn your way out of the cultural bindings of uniformity and obedience to the "proper" order being passed down in this scion of Rome's and Christendom's empire—Western Civilization—and its fear of life, death, and the transgressive (to pass over or go beyond). You will restore the balance of nature and make room for the minority, as the left-handed humans are natural, if disproportionate. You will be the ones that scout and trail-blaze the way forward-outward-over from the churning fringe of the crumbling, and unsustainable empire.

One day you will become the forest wilds—a rich ecosystem of thriving, vibrant life, sheltering both the sun-loving and shade-loving lifeforms. A life-system that integrates shadow and recycles death rather than trying to hide it and forget about it. For now, start with being the brave green of crocus and snowdrop that resists the killing and colorless snow, and finds the sun's energy even in the dark lands and through the clouded skies. Promise yourself, our society, and future generations that the good is what's sustainable and that Spring will always come again. Grow, and become the Imbolc quickening, the piercing hope in the deep of blustering Winter.

And dance with its winds.

LEFT SACRED

Works Cited

Awakening Against What's Awakened

Jung, Carl. Wotan. http://www.philosopher.eu/others-writings/essay-on-wotan-w-nietzsche-c-g-jung/ (retrieved 12/1/2016)

After Procopius

Hunt, August. *The Mysteries of Avalon: A Primer on Arthurian Druidism*. August Hunt, 2011.

Modern Sin Eaters

Estes, Clarissa Pinkola. *Women Who Run with the Wolves*. New York: Ballantine Books, 1996.

Muddy Boots and Mistletoe. "Cosmology and Compost." https://incidentaldruidry.wordpress.com/2014/01/18/on-cosmology-and-compost/

The Reawakening of Tribal Consciousness

Maalouf, Amin, *In the Name of Identity: Violence and the Need to Belong*. New York: Penguin Books, 2000.

Quinn, Daniel. *Beyond Civilization: Humanity's Next Great Adventure*. New York: Three Rivers Press, 1999.

Dobson, Andrew. *Green Political Thought* (4th ed.). New York: Routledge, 2007.

Goodman, *Paul. Growing Up Absurd*. New York: Vintage, 1960.

Badiou, Alain. *The Rebirth of History*. http://ouleft.org/wp-content/uploads/Badiou-Riots-and-Uprisings.pdf

Bodley, John H. *Cultural Anthropology: Tribes, States, and the Global System*. (5th ed.) Plymouth: Altamira, 2011.

Eckersely, Robyn. *The Green State*. Cambridge: MIT Press, 2004.

The Impure Object of the Left Sacred

Bataille, Georges. *Erotism: Death & Sensuality*. San Francisco: City Lights, 1986.

---.The Accursed Share. NY: Zone Books, 1993.

Biles, Jeremy and Kent L. Brintnall. *Negative Ecstacies: Georges Bataille and the Study of Religion*. NY: Fordham University Press, 2015.

Burkert, Walter. *Greek Religion*. Cambridge: Harvard, 1985.

Conner, Randy P. *Blossom of Bone: Reclaiming the Connections Between Homoeroticism and the Sacred*. NY: Harper Collins, 1993.

A BEAUTIFUL RESISTANCE

Direk, Zeynep. "Bataille and Kristeva on Religion." *Negative Ecstasies*. Ed. Jeremy Biles & Kent L. Brintnall. NY: Fordham UP, 2015. 182-201.

Douglas, Mary. *Purity and Danger: An Analysis of the Concepts of Pollution and Taboo*. London: Routledge & Kegan Paul, 1966.

Koch, John T. *The Celtic Heroic Age: Literary Sources for Ancient Celtic Europe and Early Ireland and Wales*. Celtic Studies Publications, 1995.

Kristeva, Julia. *Powers of Horror: An Essay on Abjection*. NY: Columbia UP, 1982.

Rabinowitz, Jacob. *The Rotting Goddess: The Origin of the Witch in Classical Antiquity*. NY: Autonomedia, 1998.

Riley, Alexander T. "'Renegade Durkheimianism' and the Transgressive/Left Sacred." Web.

Thompson, Christopher Scott. *A God Who Makes Fire: The Bardic Mysticism of Amergin*. 2013.

Gods of My Ancestors

Ignatiev, Noel. *How the Irish Became White*. Abingdon-on-Thames: Routledge, 2008

About the Artists

Li Pallas

Cover and Layout Design

Born to atheist divorcées in suburban New York, Li Pallas formed an existential sense of otherworldliness. She sees prophecy as a series of complex narratives used to interpret the human condition, illuminating the trappings of corporeal melodrama and moving us towards ethical choice. She finds meaning in talking to strangers in installations she invents, creates fine art print media as an affront to systemic narcissism, writes theory on aesthetics and intersectional justice, and moonlights as a book designer at Gods & Radicals.   bureau.lipallaslovesyou.com

Marion Le Bourhis

Untitled, p 13; Untitled, p 42, Untitled, p 59; Untitled, page 68

Marion Le Bourhis is a lesbian socialist anarchist, born in the fishermen town of Concarneau in Bretagne, France. She's lived at least ten lives already, and has been a paramedic, barmaid, social worker, and a theatre technician. She practices urbex photography, exploring abandoned places while listening to walls and their memories. Photography modifies her reality, losing herself in the world within the world of what she watches. Her camera is her anti-depressant, and liberty is her motor.

Find more at www.facebook.com/MarionLeBourhisPhoto/

Christopher DeLange

Capturing Water, p 27; Capturing Land, p 31; Capturing Fire, p 36; Capturing Smoke, p 62

Christopher DeLange is a multi-disciplined artist, living in North Carolina. Over the past 20 years he has assisted more than seven different visual artist throughout the US and Europe on a variety of creative projects. To see more of Christopher's artwork, please visit www.csdj.net

Brianna Bliss

wetlightdeep, p 19; jus de granite, p 22; death's head, p 47

Brianna Bliss is a student of archetypal language; writer, poet, artist and submitted vessel for divine intervention. She promotes Verbal Alchemy, that is, that words are magick and we heal through expression of all our parts. For pleasure she reads, dances, explodes on a page, blows glass, and explores what she can in the web of nature, life, death, and in between. See more at www.verbal-alchemy.com/

Loïs Cordelia

Spirit of Ireland - Goddess Brigid of the Triple Moons, p 5; Janus, p 66

Loïs Cordelia (born 1982, Ipswich) is a prolific UK artist and illustrator, working in diverse styles, ranging from intricate scalpel paper-cut designs to energetic acrylic speed-painting. Since 1999, she has been a studio assistant to children's illustrator Jan Pienkowski (born 1936, Warsaw), and holds a first level Honours degree in Arabic from the University of Edinburgh. Loïs' website includes a comprehensive portfolio and a dynamic record of her busy schedule of exhibitions, live art demonstrations, workshops, talks, and other events.   www.LoisCordelia.com

A BEAUTIFUL RESISTANCE

www.ingramcontent.com/pod-product-compliance
Lightning Source LLC
Chambersburg PA
CBHW042356030426

42336CB00030B/3496